SINGING T[

A layman's approach to religious music

HAROLD COPEMAN

With a preface by

BRUNO TURNER

HAROLD COPEMAN
OXFORD

Published in the United Kingdom by Harold Copeman.

May 1996.

British Library Cataloguing-in-Publication Data. A catalogue record for this book is available from the British Library.

ISBN 0 9515798 6 X

Singing the Meaning:
   A Layman's Guide to Religious Music.

Printed from author's typesetting
by Ipswich Book Co. Ltd.

Available from Harold Copeman,
22 Tawney Street, Oxford, OX4 1NJ (tel. 01865 243830).

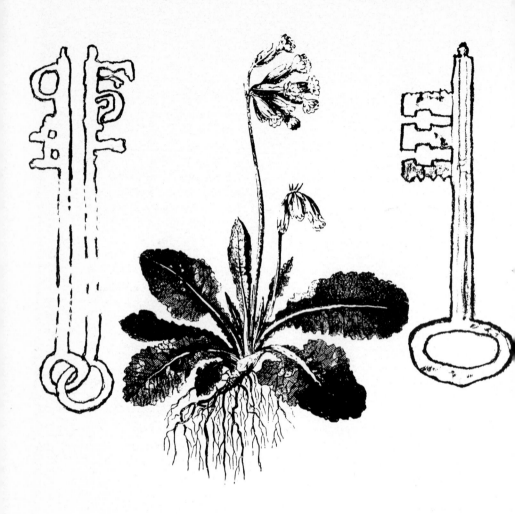

Left. Keys of Heaven, drawn from frontispiece.
Centre. Cowslip (*Primula veris*), C.A. Johns, *Flowers of the Field*, 26th edn., 1889, 514.
Right. 15th-c. key from Moorfields (*London Museum Medieval Catalogue,* 148, no. 7).
Overleaf. Illuminated page from early 12th-c. *Meditations of St Anselm*, from St Albans Abbey, MS 70 f.58v., Verdun, France. Christ hands the keys of Heaven to Simon Peter: see note opposite.

iv

KNOWING THE MEANING

A visitor from Mars looking at the frontispiece would see (if he grasped the idea of pictures at all) a short man looking at a tall man, who is looking towards and above our viewpoint. They hold two keys; two sheep look up at the tall man.

Most of us will recognise at least part of the meaning of these symbols. In the early twelfth century the Anglo-Norman reader of the *Meditations of St Anselm* would have no doubt of the imagery: Christ, towering over the obeisant Simon Peter as he hands him the keys of heaven and points to the sheep, who are the Church, saying (in Latin; there were of course no vernacular bibles) 'Feed my lambs' (John, 21, 15). That reader would also know that Christ used the name Peter to denote the Rock (Greek *petros*) on which Christ would found the Church (Matthew 16, 18f); that Peter would have power on earth which would have effect in heaven; and the Church's teaching that Peter's authority as Pope and first Bishop of Rome passed to all later Popes.

The souls and minds of the sheep of the Church were to receive their nourishment exclusively, in the form of the apostolic faith, from the Pope's bishops and priests. Entry to heaven and salvation from everlasting torment would depend on good standing with Peter's successors.

We may notice that Christ is so tall (a symbol for his Divine nature) that he cannot fit within the frame which holds Peter, though they are both men. Conceivably the two sheep represent the Western and Eastern Churches, the latter turning its back on Peter and Rome: but this is no doubt too far-fetched.

The Reformation did not extinguish the absorption of religious images into popular thought and language. The drawings opposite show Peter's keys of heaven and a late medieval key from London, and what in German is the *Himmelsschlüsselblume*, the 'Key of Heaven flower', the Cowslip, one name for which is 'Our Lady's bunch of keys'. In his 'St John Passion' Bach has the cowslip growing through the Crown of Thorns, and (evidently referring to a current legend) sees the red spots on the cowslip as drops of Christ's blood; this image yields the intense but obscure text of the bass Arioso, no. 31, p. 148.

v

AUTHOR'S NOTE

I have been fortunate in finding people who were willing to read all or part of my subjective musings and to make helpful suggestions and remove errors. I owe thanks to Keith Bennett, Margaret Bent, John Fenton, Jennie and John Macquarrie, James Mark, Charles Mitchell-Innes, John Randall, Emma Tristram: and to those who have sung round my table and argued about the texts we have been singing, sacred and secular.

I am most grateful to Bruno Turner for his Preface; to the Revd. Professor John Macquarrie for permission to include the text of his sermon on Judgment, Heaven and Hell (Appendix 3); to Martin Kauffmann of the Bodleian Library for suggesting the frontispiece as a depiction of the keys of Heaven; to Mme Ben Lakhdar-Kreuwen, of the Bibliothèque Municipale, Verdun, for the transparency and for permission to reproduce it; and to Arthur MacGregor of the Ashmolean Museum for guiding me through medieval keys.

My drafts of this book have benefited from repeated and most perceptive scrutiny of style and matter from Richard Jeffery and Helen Mead; remaining infelicities are mine.

Edward and Jeremy James and Steve Lasenby have patiently helped me to tame the computer.

Harold Copeman
Oxford, April 1996.

CONTENTS

PREFACE by BRUNO TURNER

Harold Copeman has set out to satisfy a need that is often ignored or passed over with little thought. The need is to provide a bridge of comprehension (not necessarily of agreement nor of close empathy) that would span a gulf of ignorance of, or indifference to, the texts of sacred music. This book is intended to help singers and listeners alike to find a way under the formidable carapace of ecclesiastical Latin and the archaic forms of our heritage of religious music.

As Copeman warns, this is not the book for you if, already, you know it all as an educated believer or rejecter. Others may consider it irrelevant to try to understand the meaning and function of the liturgical or devotional texts; the music may seem self-sufficient, enthralling purely as sound.

Those of us, now elderly, educated in the 1930s and 1940s, recall a world without 'early music' and without religious ecumenism. Most Roman Catholics derided Anglicans as woolly-minded, neither Catholic nor fully Protestant; Anglicans, however High, disliked the arrogant triumphalism, the rigidity and centralisation of Roman authority in a despotic Papacy. Non-conformists, Copeman tells me, kept carefully away from both these worlds.

When I emerged from a very strict Roman Catholic family and from a rigorous Jesuit education, I stood blinking in the harsh light of post-war realities, blinking but unafraid: we were right; the rest were wrong. Protestants were heretics. I recall my father's concern when I met and mixed with Anglican church musicians. Sir Richard Terry had referred to Dom Anselm Hughes (of the Anglican Benedictine Order) as 'the bogus monk'.

Things are different now. Thirty years after Vatican II, the Roman Church fights fitfully the onslaught of scientific discovery and the march of information-fuelled rationalism (without any detectable increase in wisdom as distinct from knowledge). The Catholic liturgy is in tatters, abandoned by its custodians. Ceremonial worship, elaborate liturgies, the universal Latin, the sacraments and contemplative prayer are neglected if not abolished. A few notable institutions keep a celebration of the Mass with integral liturgical music (rather than what is often a *missa cum strepitu* - mass-with-noises-off); but in general the great year-round cycle of the Offices of the Roman Rite has disappeared from the Catholic world.

Yet, the interest in religious art remains high. Gregorian chants, the most strictly liturgical of all music, have fascinated young and old alike, hit the charts, and are encapsulated on shiny discs, divorced from the ceremonial worship for which they were composed and in which they exclusively existed, many for a thousand years. Ripped from their proper places, in which they were fully understood in their function as sung prayer, they now reside like coffee-table art books or as *objets trouvées* like the stolen or rescued *retablos* from Spanish chapels that stand forlorn in the Victoria and Albert Museum.

Magnificent, yes. Beautiful, yes, and touching the heart and mind, yes indeed. But functionless, de-contextualised - such cold words pointing to the true heart and soul of the original purposes.

Polyphony, and the other generalised classifications we now give to varieties of once-living music, has had this fate. It's a new world of resuscitation of old things. There is, for many performers and for the commercial chain through to the listener-customers, a real future in making the past into the present, fleeting though the latter may be.

It is this brave new world of early music that needs so very badly the bridge-building that Harold Copeman has offered in this book.

Historical awareness, the cautious but admonitory phrase that has supplanted the dreadful foolhardiness of 'Authenticity', must surely include comprehension by performers and listeners alike of the meaning and the significance of the ceremonial and liturgical functions in their bedrock foundations of religious belief, doctrines and dogma on which the Christian heritage of sacred music was built.

To appreciate, to empathise with, to be moved by the image of Mary the mother weeping at the feet of her crucified son is one thing. To feel with our forebears that the persons were *the* Mother and her Son, God Incarnate, is quite another. *Stabat Mater dolorosa iuxta crucem lacrimosa* can and does move composers yet again to set the text, and moves all of us to be at one in the public manifestation of personal grief that it genuinely represents.

It is not so easy, in our Age, to get past the Latin and into the full meaning of St Thomas Aquinas's hymns for Corpus Christi, which enunciate - with triumphant confidence - the Catholic dogma of Eucharistic Transubstantiation. But *Pange lingua gloriosi corporis mysterium* ... and *Sacris solemniis* ... were for real - the literal truth for Catholics, over the centuries, about the sacred banquet in which Christ's body and blood are consumed by the faithful.

To believe, as it was believed, that the liturgical services of worship were communal (or private) divine praise, enactments of truths, cannot now be expected of institutions that offer little more than the nominal hallowing of charitable works.

The question of sincerity cannot be evaded. We could not possibly summon together the performers needed for Elgar's *Dream of Gerontius* if we relied only upon those who subscribe to the doctrines contained in Cardinal Newman's poem. But we do need to understand and to convey with apparent conviction the inner meaning of whatever is being performed, just as the best actors do in their roles.

...

This is all very admonitory. The leavening of a little levity will do no harm. Marx (Groucho, not Karl) had it right. Or was it S.J. Perelman behind him? Honesty and integrity are what you need, and if you can fake *them*, you've got it made. (If ...)

Turre, Almeria, 1996

1. WHO SINGS, AND WHY?

In the irreligious late twentieth century many thousands of singers spend time, energy and money singing religious music. Out of these, I guess that in this country several hundred make a living out of it; others record or broadcast it, and tens of thousands listen to the results; and a few devote their lives to intensive research and writing about it.

This is peculiar. Has the western world been gripped by religious mania? Have the churches overflowed with worshippers attracted by the beauty, or the emotional force, of the music of the church service?

The answer must be No. A few churches overflow for special occasions like a carol service, or for a concert which has nothing to do with the regular worship: but it is (at the least) uncommon to find a church where the enormous heritage of religious music is treated by clergy and laymen as part of the worship, intelligently chosen and competently performed.

To provide live music at the standard that people demand in a recorded performance would of course be vastly expensive and often inappropriate, though much can be done if competent amateurs and professionals get together (on whatever terms) to provide music for worship.

Many church choirs have disappeared because neither young nor old want to accept regular commitments to practise and to attend services, and also because the 'liturgical movement' has emphasised the congregation's part in the service and reduced that of the choir. At the same time the Anglican Matins, for which much fine music was written for dignified and treasured words, has widely been displaced by 'parish communion' (often with unworthy music) or by informal 'family services'. Evensong has faded away in most parish churches; and nearly everywhere in the Roman Catholic Church the immense repertory of Latin music has been dropped. In non-conformist churches and chapels the regular performance of oratorio or cantata has declined.

Yet there is an insatiable demand for concert performances of *Messiah*, whether amateur or professional; and many singers are strongly drawn towards Continental and British motets and masses, particularly from 1500 to 1700, and to works never heard until the post-war years - notably the Monteverdi *Vespers of 1610*. For reasonably competent singers these works not only provide a challenge - often met with great confidence and verve - but evidently feed an emotional and aesthetic hunger. In recent years the standard of the best choirs and of professional specialists has improved sensationally, and is admired overseas. An immense range of recondite music appears in recorded form.

Cathedral and college chapel choirs have played an important part, and have generated conductors and leading singers who have stimulated good performances in cities and country places, sometimes in glorious buildings under-used for centuries. Much of this movement, however, is unconnected with the practice of formal religion. My strong impression, from fifty-odd years of singing in choirs and conducting them, is that very many singers have grown up not only without a liturgical tradition but without much background knowledge of the Bible or of orthodox Christianity: indeed, I find that thinking about the music's text constantly shows up my own ignorance. Those who never feel this are perhaps reading the wrong book.

The music with which we are concerned sprang from a culture of intense religious belief and observance. Until the seventeenth century, at least, religion was a much greater part of life, in town or country, than in most societies today. Experiences of life and religion permeated each other; death was familiar through violence, famine and disease, and the fires and torments that could follow death were vivid in the teachings, paintings and stained glass of the Church. The call for mercy was no formality; the congregation were persuaded that a favourable response from a heavenly authority demanded acceptance of the faith and teachings of the Church, and intercession to Christ through the Church and the saints, especially the Blessed Virgin Mary.

The manner in which people worshipped often depended not on personal convictions but on the preference of their ruler; kingdoms might be converted from paganism, and, later, switched between Protestantism and Catholicism because of the ruler's convictions or his political convenience. When the Court of Saxony became Catholic, to support the claim of Friedrich Augustus I to the Polish throne in 1697, the people of Saxony remained Protestant: but this was a new phenomenon.

Much of the music was written for the Roman Catholic Church, some for continental Protestant Churches, for Scottish Presbyterian and for English and Welsh non-conformist Churches. (I am not attempting to comment on the music of the Orthodox Churches nor on Jewish and other religious music.)

The medieval Church's music was written by professionals, who might hold an ecclesiastical rank as priests, minor clergy or monks. Their lives, and careers, lay in enhancing formal worship with their compositions and

3

performances. Whether in a monastery, a cathedral or a chapel of a college or court, they were normally part of a team devoted to performing a liturgy to the glory of God, and conveying this to their hearers, whether those were a few colleagues in the chancel or a lay congregation in the nave. In the Catholic Church, as Pope Pius X said in his *Motu proprio* of St Cecilia's Day 1903, a lay choir was a substitute for the choir of clerics, with 'a really liturgical office'. He went on to explain that this was why women couldn't sing in the choir!

Especially before the Reformation, composers and singers would understand the words of their music in accordance with the teaching of the Church at the time. Their outlook is far from ours; I pursue this in Chapter 4. The words of the music may sometimes relate to a literal truth, or they may be using traditional and poetic imagery, perhaps to arouse faith and teach the Church's doctrines. How do we place this fifteenth-century carol?

1. There is no rose of such virtue
    As is the rose that bare Jesu.
        Alleluia.
2. For in this rose contained was
    Heaven and earth in little space;
        Res miranda.   [A thing to be wondered at]
3. By this rose we may well see
    That he is God in persons three,
        Pari forma.   [Of equal form; of the same
                                substance, equal in importance]
4. The angels sungen the shepherds to:
    Gloria in excelsis Deo:
        Gaudeamus.   [Let us rejoice]
5. Leave we all this worldly mirth,
    And follow we this joyful birth;
        Transeamus.   [Let us make this transition]

Verses 2 and 3 expound theological points in terms of the historical birth of Jesus: Mary, the rose (without a thorn), bore in her womb Jesus, who was to be both God and man; and (in this miraculous process) the three persons of the Trinity are seen - God in his fatherhood, the Holy Spirit through whose agency Mary conceived, and the Son (to be born as the Word incarnate). Verses 4 and 5 are exhortations to the faithful hearer: to rejoice, and to accept and undergo a change of life ('repentance'). The whole is carried by poetic language which looks back to the medieval vogue of courtly love, with its closed garden, and applies this to the veneration of the Virgin Mary (C.S. Lewis discusses this in *The Allegory of Love*, esp. 8, 20). We get nowhere if we read the words in only one linguistic dimension.

The differences in kind between various texts may not always be so obvious. We can easily take too literally a story preserved by an oral story-telling people, or a poem which makes its point by metaphor rather than by common-sense usage. If we find incredible the story of Gabriel's Annunciation, for instance, we can easily reject the whole of the underlying religious belief. This may be a terrible waste, based on a misunderstanding of the nature of the story, and perhaps a reaction against a fundamentalist belief in the literal truth of every word of Scripture. My own instinct is that though there is much that our honest thought-processes rebel against, there is an important task of translation into concepts that we can understand and defend: for the germ of the faith is a pearl that we must not lose or lightly reject.

There is a further impediment too when the words are in other languages, usually medieval Latin or early modern German. We are often tempted to sing the notes as if we know what the text is all about, while having a vague idea at best. Publishers' translations may not adequately illuminate the meaning, but choirs often include linguists who can act as textual critics.

Often singers skid over the attractive surface of the music, unconscious of the demands and the terrors of the religion which it served; this may mean missing the musical sense as well as the textual. In Britain most of us can begin to feel the force of the text in Protestant services - for instance, Bach's *Passions*, and *Messiah* - but ancient Catholic texts (as in the carol quoted above) may be less immediately approachable. This book attempts to suggest ways to get a little closer to what devout church musicians had in their minds and hearts at the time the music was new and in liturgical use, so that we can penetrate the music a little more deeply for ourselves.

Big questions will come to the mind of the reader: what are we doing, anyway, singing ancient religious music in a later and more secular age? Can we harmonise it with honest expression of our own religion - or lack of it? When we sing a Bach cantata in a concert, may the experience communicated to the audience, and to us, be of a religious kind; and if so, is there a sharp distinction from what happens when it is sung in a service? Is this quite different when the work is a Mass? May our musical performance provoke changes in our personal religion (or lack of it), and affect our hearers' lives too? It would be arid to be faced with a series of essays on these points: instead, *solvitur ambulando* - let ideas emerge as these chapters develop.

I write this book as a seeker for the germ of the faith, not as a propagandist for the beliefs I attempt to describe, though I have tried at some points to make my own position clear. What I am able to say about religion may appear somewhat detached, but I hope some readers will find grains of enlightenment and even of encouragement: and that none will find the core of their faith disturbed. We need, I suggest, to preserve mystery but to reduce mystification and confusion. On balance I echo Goethe's plea in his reputed last words, *Mehr Licht.*

2. THE STORY SO FAR

In the 1990s there is perhaps a place for a short connected account of what used to be common background - the events of the Bible and the growth of the Church. What follows is obviously incomplete, but it may serve as a departure point for thought and reading: and I mention in this context a few familiar musical works. (Readers with a religious education may wish to skip several pages.) A section in the Bibliography on page 171 suggests a few among the many thousands of possible books.

Versions of the Bible
I give this account in the terms which have been familiar over the centuries; in Chapter 3 I shall attempt to explain, to readers who find Christian assumptions and traditions unfamiliar or baffling, what some of the traditional concepts have meant. My biblical quotations are from the 'Authorised Version' (1611); there are good modern versions, particularly *The Revised English Bible* (Oxford and Cambridge, 1989), but the *AV* has a special place in English music, together with the Psalms in the *Book of Common Prayer* (1662, drawing on Coverdale's version in the 1549 *BCP*).

The Old Testament (OT)
This first part, 973 pages in my copy, tells the history of the Jews, the 'chosen people' with whom Jehovah made a covenant or testament. The worship of a multiplicity of gods or idols was to cease, and Jehovah, or Yahweh, 'I am who I am', was to be recognised as the One God, who was the Lord God of the nation Israel.

The first of the OT's thirty-nine Books, **Genesis**, relates how the world and all life came from an initial creative act of will by God (Haydn, 'The Creation'; Copland, 'In the Beginning'). The account of the creation in ch. 1 is followed by a different version in ch. 2, vv. 4-7. Here, 'man became a living soul', so he had a will which was free (in all I write He embraces She, especially in the Garden of Eden). Chs. 2-3 tell of Adam, Eve and the serpent, and of man's first disobedience, Adam's Fall, from which all generations inherited their proneness to sin, or Original Sin.

After many generations, of fantastic longevity, God punished, by drowning in the Flood, all living things except for Noah's family and two of each sort of animal (chs. 6-9; Britten's 'Noye's Fludde'). When the waters subsided God made a covenant with Noah, his sons 'and with your seed after you ... and every living creature that is with you' that 'the waters shall no more become a flood to destroy all flesh'. The token of this covenant would be the rainbow.

In chs. 11-12 we come to the patriarch Abraham. God told him to move his family from Mesopotamia (now Iraq) to Canaan, later known as Palestine, and promised, despite the native Canaanites' claim, to give the land to Abraham's seed for ever ('et semini ejus in secula' at the end of *Magnificat*). This undertaking, of course, has had enduring consequences in Middle East politics; indeed, ch. 15 defined the gift of land as extending, inter alia, from the Nile to the Euphrates. Abraham's wife, who was barren, gave Abraham her maid as wife; she bore Ishmael, who, God promises, would beget twelve princes, 'and I will make him a great nation' (chs. 16-17).

God repeated his covenant, demanded circumcision of all men and male children, and promised a child to

Abraham and his first wife Sarah (whose ages were 100 and 90). The child was Isaac; God tested Abraham's faith and obedience (ch. 22) by demanding that he sacrifice his son. After Abraham had agreed and was about to kill Isaac, the angel of the Lord ordered him to desist, and a ram caught in a thicket was killed and burnt instead (Britten, 'Abraham and Isaac').

Iaaac's son Jacob tricked his brother Esau out of his birthright (ch. 25 and 27); his father's anger made him return for many years to Haran in Mesopotamia, where he married two sisters, and had twelve sons by them and their maids; the marital arrangements are described in some detail in chs. 29 and 30.

On Jacob's journey back to Haran he met a mysterious stranger with whom he wrestled during the night; this evidently divine or angelic figure told him to take the name Israel ('He that striveth with God'), 'for as a prince hast thou power with God and with men, and hast prevailed': ch. 32. (Names can have strong meanings, and be potent in use.) Before Israel died he appointed his sons to be the twelve tribes of Israel (ch. 49). His son Judah's tribe came to form the southern kingdom, which included Jerusalem. (The name Israel is variously applied in the OT, sometimes to the whole of the Jewish people but also to the ten northern tribes as opposed to Judah.)

Jacob's youngest and favourite son was Joseph, who (ch. 37) after an ambush by his brothers was sold into captivity 'for twenty pieces of silver', and taken into Egypt, where he served a captain of Pharaoh's, and was imprisoned on a false accusation by Pharaoh's wife of attempted rape (ch. 39). When Joseph interpreted a dream of the king as warning of seven years of plenty followed by seven years of dearth, and suggested what to do about it, he was made governor, and Egypt prospered (ch. 41). Israel and his sons, his flocks and herds, also came to settle in Egypt, at first with generous support from the king but later under persecution (chs. 42-50, Exodus 1).

Moses, from the Levite tribe, who was found as a baby in the bulrushes by Pharaoh's daughter, was appointed by the Lord God, speaking from the burning bush that was not consumed (Exodus 2-3), to lead the children of Israel out of exile in Egypt. To force Pharaoh to 'let my people go' (a spiritual in Tippett's 'A Child of our Time') the Lord brought plagues and disasters to Egypt (Handel's 'Israel in Egypt'). He ordered the Israelites through Moses to mark their doorways on a certain night with the blood of a sacrificed lamb, which they were to eat that night, staying indoors (ch. 12). For seven days they were to eat only unleavened bread. The bloodmark was to show the Lord which houses to pass over when he came to destroy all the first-born of Egypt; and this Passover was to be kept each year for ever. (The Bach 'Passions' tell how, many centuries later, Christ decided to hold his Last Supper on the first day of this feast before he was to be betrayed and crucified (Matthew 26); the Jewish authorities wanted to avoid taking and killing him at this particular time 'lest there be an uproar among the people'. And we note the way the imagery of the lamb and its blood lived through to have a new meaning.)

After the killing of the first-born the Egyptians were glad to be rid of the children of Israel, who went off into the desert towards Canaan, 'six hundred thousand on foot that were men, beside children'. God moved Pharaoh to pursue them, but his army was defeated, and the Israelites escaped across a miraculously-parted Red Sea (Exodus 14).

11

Through Moses God made known his commandments for the Jewish people on Mount Sinai; Exodus 19-24 and later books record these laws in great detail, and their importance for Jews has endured. Long instructions for ritual worship follow.

Then we read of the actions and teachings of a long succession of prophets, priests and kings, Joshua, Samuel, Saul, David (c.1000 BC) and Handel's Zadok the priest. David's son Solomon (more Handel) built the grandiose Temple, designed to make Jerusalem a worthy capital for a great power, described in 1 Kings 6; he 'loved many strange women', and he had 700 wives and 300 concubines (ch. 11).

In the late tenth century BC the northern tribes revolted against the House of David (the monarchs reigning in Jerusalem), and it was they who retained the name 'Israel'. The country was unstable and in 721 BC the Assyrians captured and exiled its people. In the southern part of the Jewish kingdom, 'Judah', the throne continued to pass from father to son in the line of David. The kings made unwise alliances against invasion, against the advice of the prophet Isaiah, and in 586 BC Nebuchadnezzar destroyed Jerusalem and Solomon's Temple, the unique centre of Jewish worship, and took captives to Babylon. From their long exile (from which they were released in 538 BC by Cyrus of Persia) arose the Lamentations of Jeremiah, set to music by several composers, and Ps. 137, 'By the waters of Babylon' (Palestrina's evocative *Super flumina Babylonis*). The Second Temple was built in 520 BC under Persian rule, which lasted until 330 BC when Alexander, King of Macedon (in northern Greece), captured much of the Middle East; by this time the OT period had ended.

The **Psalms**, written over several centuries, are poems of devotional prayer, which became the hymn-book of the Second Temple. They extend right across the Jewish nation's response to God; I consider them in Chapter 7.

After the Old Testament

After Alexander's death Palestine, the area of the 'Holy Land', passed to the Macedonian and Syrian Seleucids; Judas Maccabaeus (Handel's subject) led a successful revolt by the Jews and restored the desecrated Temple in 165 BC, and a dynasty of Jewish priest-kings followed until in 64 BC Pompey conquered the country for the Romans. The Temple survived until it was destroyed by the Romans in AD 70; synagogue worship, more limited in its nature, had begun in the Exile and has continued ever since. In the centuries immediately before Christ the Jewish law was developed by scribes, rabbis and later by the Pharisees; it became rigid and all-embracing.

The New Testament (OT)

This part of the Bible is shorter (297 pages) than the OT. It opens with the four Gospels, written two or three generations after the birth of Jesus in about 4 BC in Nazareth, in Galilee in the north of Palestine. The Western Church celebrates the Christ-mass on 25 December; one intention was to divert the people from the popular twelve days of pagan Yule. In earthly terms Jesus was the child of humble parents, Joseph and Mary: but also, in theological terms, he was the Son of God through the action of the Holy Spirit. The archangel Gabriel explained this to the Virgin Mary at the Annunciation (Lady Day, 25 March, nine months before the birth); Mary's response is the *Magnificat*. We are very familiar with musical expressions

13

of the joy of Christmas, sometimes tinged with the bitter myrrh of what is to come; and we sing of the mystery of the birth of God's Son in lowliness among the animals in *O magnum mysterium,* set by Victoria, Byrd, G. Gabrieli and Poulenc.

In his manhood Jesus was baptised in the River Jordan by John the Baptist, who had been sent to 'make straight the way of the Lord', as we know from Gibbons's 'This is the record of John'; the Holy Spirit appeared as a dove. This is recorded by St John the Evangelist in his Gospel, ch. 1, 19-34; he adds 'as said the prophet Esaias' - Isaiah - so as to set the event in Jewish history, and to authenticate Jesus as the promised Messiah - or, in Greek, 'Christ'. Jesus then survived the Temptations (Mark 1, 9-13), and went on to preach a new gospel of love and personal sacrifice, performing miracles and gathering a small band of disciples. This brought conflict with both the Roman authorities and the Jewish High Priests (around AD 30).

After the anguished meditation of his Passion (singers will know Bach's settings of the Gospels of St Matthew and St John) Jesus was tried, executed by crucifixion, buried, and rose again on the third day, Easter Sunday.

He then visited and surprised the mourning disciples, and their lives were transformed. With enormous energy and endurance they obeyed the command to tell the story to others, starting with the Jews but soon extending their evangelism to the Gentiles (that is, all non-Jews, largely the Greek-speaking people of the Mediterranean, then the Romans themselves). Jesus himself ascended to his Father in heaven; ten days later, on the Jewish Pentecost which Christians adopted as Whitsunday, the Holy Ghost (the Holy Spirit of God) descended on the disciples with tongues of fire, to give them the inspiration and the

14

guidance that they had from Christ while he was on earth: Acts, 2, the continuation of St Luke's Gospel which covers the journeys from Palestine to spread Christianity. (Music for these occasions is mentioned in Appendix 1.)

A few years after the Crucifixion Saul of Tarsus, who had been serving the Romans in oppressing the Jews, underwent a dramatic and painful conversion on the road to Damascus (Acts 9), and became 'Paul', a leader and theologian of the Church. The NT includes (out of historical order, after the Gospels) several Epistles by Paul and others - letters to the churches which the scattered converts founded - which develop his doctrine. In I Corinthians 15 he gives the earliest account of the Resurrection.

A generation or more later, the four Gospel accounts of the life and teaching of Jesus were written by (or in the names of) Matthew, Mark (the earliest), Luke and John. Luke also wrote the Acts of the Apostles, covering the journeys to spread the Gospel. ('Apostles' refers to the twelve disciples, but also to later evangelists.)

The Revelation of St John the Divine, the last book in the Bible, contains an extraordinary series of visions of the end of the world, leading to a new heaven and a new earth, and 'the holy city, new Jerusalem, coming down from God out of heaven, prepared as a bride adorned for her husband' (ch. 21, 1f); it is also the source of some of the text of 'Messiah' (notably 'Worthy is the Lamb' and the Amen chorus (ch. 5, 12f).

The Apocrypha

In the Septuagint, the Greek translation of the Hebrew OT, thirteen books were included which later were excluded from the Hebrew bible. They appear also in the

Latin bible, the Vulgate; in English bibles they are omitted, or included as a separate section.

The Church

At first the scattered church congregations, meeting in houses, faced persecution from the Roman authorities: but by the early fourth century the Emperor Constantine adopted Christianity and sought to unite the Church to his secular state, and to replace the pagan gods. He negotiated a doctrinal settlement with the bishops at the Council of Nicaea; from this and later Ecumenical Councils the catholic Creeds developed. Constantine moved his capital from Rome to the New Rome, Constantinople (the old Byzantium and the present Istanbul).

The senior bishops were now those of Rome, Constantinople, Alexandria and Antioch. The Bishop of Rome (seen in his church as the successor to the disciple St Peter, the Rock on whom Christ was to build his Church - Palestrina's *Tu es Petrus*) gradually became known as the Pope, and the Bishop of Constantinople as the Ecumenical Patriarch (meaning 'of the whole inhabited world'). As Rome and Constantinople drew apart over questions of doctrine and organisation, the Catholic Church in the West and the Orthodox Church in the East developed in their own ways, Alexandria and Antioch remaining important centres of Eastern evangelism.

By now the Church, no longer secret or illegal, had substantial buildings in which to worship. It survived further periods of persecution; and after the collapse of the Roman Empire in the West under attack from northern barbarians, the bishops in Gaul managed to maintain worship and some elements of civilised government. Here and in the Iberian and Italian parts of the Empire some of the invading tribes were converted, and absorbed Roman ways and local versions of Latin (see my *Singing in Latin*, ch. 2).

Missionaries from Rome, Asia Minor and North Africa continued to evangelise, and later the German parts east of the Roman frontier were converted by Irish and Anglo-Saxon missionaries.

In Gaul the Merovingian invaders started the long process of civil and religious reconstruction, and Charlemagne, a Frank from western Germany, determined to rule over a state which would be based on the Catholic religion; the Pope made him Holy Roman Emperor. With the help of the English scholar Alcuin, Charlemagne set up schools for the clergy and reformed the liturgy and reintroduced Latin; the everyday Romance dialects slowly developed into the French, Italian, Spanish and other languages. At this stage church music took the form of chant (in Latin), which continued being composed for many centuries; this, together with several centuries of polyphonic music and the concerted music of the 17th-20th centuries, provides the Catholic Church with its enormous musical repertory.

From early medieval times the Church became firmly institutionalised, with a practical monopoly of learning and administrative ability. It acquired property on a massive scale; luxury and abuse became common. Movements towards drastic reform emerged in the formation of monastic Orders; when these in turn turned to abuse and slackness, other Orders with stricter discipline grew up.

Churches and monasteries grew rich through property ownership and through pressure on rich laymen to improve their prospects in a future life by making endowments. This eventually led to pressure from rulers

who were short of money and from 'Protestant' religious
reformers. The English 'reformation', starting in the 1530s,
involved confiscation of monastic property and the
forbidding of certain religious practices. For the irrelevant
reason of Henry VIII's divorce the Church of England
became separated from Rome; and drastic reform of the
liturgy under the 1549 Act of Uniformity introduced the
services in English in the Book of Common Prayer,
designed to be heard and understood (and requiring new
musical settings). In the 1560s the Roman Catholic Church
also moved to simpler music, giving clarity to the (Latin)
words. By then Luther, Calvin and others had built up
reformed churches in Germany, Switzerland and France,
and in 1568 Philip II of Spain (Mary Tudor's widower)
started a war in the Low Countries, the home of Franco-
Flemish music, to crush the new Protestantism; this lasted
for eighty years.

Except for Mary's reign in 1553-58 the Church of
England remained a Protestant episcopal church, with a
strong blend of traditional clerical and popular Catholicism
- though during the Commonwealth in the mid-
seventeenth century it narrowly escaped losing its bishops
and being made Presbyterian. Roman Catholics were
subject to restriction or worse; many went to the Continent
in the sixteenth century until their emancipation in the
eighteenth and early nineteenth centuries. Others,
including several aristocratic families, remained as
'recusants'; this is the background to Byrd's later music.
Attempts by the papacy and Philip II to reclaim England
through Jesuit missionaries failed, but intensified the
oppression of the remaining Catholics.

France remained mainly Catholic, but suffered
religious wars and later developed a strong anti-clerical

movement. In the French revolution there was drastic action against the Church; Cambrai Cathedral, where Dufay had served, the greatest church in the Western world, was taken to pieces and used for building stone. Italy, Spain and Portugal remain Catholic. Germany and Switzerland, and also Ireland, still remain divided between Protestantism and Catholicism. So does the Netherlands, formed by revolution against its occupation and religious oppression by Catholic Spain.

The religious music we now sing comes not only from the Roman Catholic, Lutheran and Anglican traditions, but from the great store of hymns whose words and music often grew in English and Welsh Protestant non-conformist churches and from Scottish metrical versions of the Psalms (see Chapter 7); from translations of early Latin hymns, often under the influence of the Anglo-Catholic 'Oxford Movement' of the last century; and by absorption of popular melodies from many countries - folk-song, Lutheran hymns, French psalms and carols, and Negro spirituals. Unfortunately some churches, not just in England, have used for their rewritten liturgies a faded pseudo-pop style of music. Much of the repertory of both Latin and English music has fallen into disuse - but we have to recall that historically most music quickly fell out of fashion and was replaced; the revival of older music is a habit of the last two centuries, which has now snowballed.

Recently the style of chant through which the Eastern Orthodox Churches have worshipped in an unbroken tradition has had a sudden burst of musical attention through the works of Arvo Pärt and John Tavener. In this book, however, I limit myself to the music of the western traditions.

19

3. BASICS OF FAITH,
FOR NON-CHRISTIANS

What is religion about, and is it akin to philosophy or science, or to folk-lore: and how does emotion fit in? Some readers will be entirely confident of the answer: this chapter is for the others.

The concept of God

Let us start with an important area of confusion: what do we mean when we use the word 'God' - and what was meant at the time our music was written?

We will clear away the evasive objection that God is so infinite, remote, mysterious (or whatever) that definition is impossible, or else that it is impious to try to bring God down to the level of human understanding. If we use a word, in our own thought or writing or in converse with others, there must be understanding of how that word is to be applied and understood: otherwise there is no sure meeting of minds, and what we say may be taken to mean something we did not intend. It is easy to drift into using the word with inconsistent meanings, and fool ourselves and deceive or confuse others.

I will take the word 'God' as denoting the being that created the world and our lives. Starting from this simple definition - which is, to repeat, quite different from an attempted description of God - we can then make statements about God, the being: for instance, that the power of God is infinite, and that it is (or is not) exercised at all times and in all places. (Did God - as some people seem genuinely to have believed - cause York Minster to be struck by lightning and partly destroyed by fire because a controversial Bishop of Durham had recently been consecrated there?) Or we may wish to say that God's love is all-encompassing and/or infinite; or to relate his wondrous words and acts. (Or, having defined the word 'God', we can, if we wish, maintain that there is no God of that kind.)

What is belief?

Statements like these are major articles of belief, and must involve leaps of faith. One cannot prove that God, the all-powerful, is the all-good, let alone that good will triumph over evil: of course, if a statement can be factually demonstrated or logically proved, there is no leap of faith nor reliance on faith.

There is, however, a practical test. Faith can transform the way we live and act, and face the hardships and uncertainties of the physical world. If we have faith in the power of love we act as a channel for it in the world; and love can dissolve evil. This can be seen and believed when it actually happens, and the actual lives of Christians are the best witness and the most convincing demonstration of their belief: the leap of faith is not entirely blind.

The Old and New Covenants

Long before Christ, in Old Testament days, polytheism among the Israelites gave way to belief in one God, Yahweh, 'I am who I am'. He - for God as the supreme source of power was conventionally regarded as male - was seen as the God of the Jewish nation ('Israel', the name for the undivided nation), covenanting earthly blessings to his chosen people in return for their obedience. But the field of God's action was broadened when, in the eighth century BC, he commanded the prophet Jonah to rescue the Assyrians in Nineveh from their sins; when Jonah tried to

21

escape this awkward job by taking a boat bound for the other end of the Mediterranean, he ran into trouble with a whale. This would have been the first mission to the Gentiles; gradually God's care came to be seen as no longer being limited to the Jews.

The belief of Christians (at any rate after the first few years) was that Christ, the Incarnate Son of God, had brought the new revelation that God was the Father of all people, and that the gospel must be carried outside Jewry. The recompenses of a new Covenant were not to be material, like the OT land flowing with milk and honey (Joshua 5, 6): instead, St John conceived God as light, life and love - that is, he taught that God the Creator had these attributes, and that we can know him by knowing Christ. By a gift of Divine grace, Death had been conquered, Christ was living, and (after repentance) the Kingdom of God was already here.

Christian faith

From Christ's time faith rested in a known and loved person who was both earthly and of God, who suffered and died as a sacrifice to redeem man from his fallen state and from death and condemnation, triumphed over death in his Resurrection, and remains present with us, most especially at the celebration of Holy Communion, or 'Eucharist', or 'Mass'.

The strength and warmth of that loving faith has sustained the Church in all its branches, despite persecution, since the original direct witness by the disciples. The music that we are drawn to sing was written for this faith, and it was expressed in the regular worship of the assembled Church. (Chapter 4 will attempt to get a little closer to the outlook of medieval singers and worshippers, and Chapter 6 looks at the subsequent period.)

God: Person or abstraction?

In the scriptures God is seen from the beginning as a Person in an anthropomorphic sense - more than an abstraction like a world-force or a first cause or indeed love itself. Perhaps something of this can be grasped (even by non-believers) if we have a sense of gratitude for life and love; if we have a sense of beauty and some chance to enjoy it; or if we feel that achievements are not wholly our own doing. And reactions like gratitude, praise and adoration only make sense if they are directed towards a being - a person - who can choose and will to favour us in these ways; and rather similarly for our basic sense of obligation.

None of this proves anything about God's existence or imputed attributes: it is a sorting-out of our long-term emotional response to the world, and that no doubt depends on our upbringing and circumstances. Perhaps the happy, healthy and prosperous can more easily feel positive about existence - and those who feel confident about God's support when they are in trouble (about which there will be much to say in Chapter 4). We have a strong tendency, not confined to the faithful, to be glad to find someone to blame when things go wrong. These feelings are often aimed at God; or, in earlier times especially, at the Devil or his evil spirits.

It is natural for us to ask why things go wrong with the world: and, indeed, why does nature so often work so that things put themselves right? It is not always clear what sort of an answer we expect: but I suggest that in asking 'Why?' about our world or our existence we are unconsciously assuming that there is a purpose and a power to be enquired about, and therefore a mind and a will behind the universe. 'Why X?' means something like 'What purpose lay behind the decision that X should happen?' (this is different from the (scientific and impersonal) question 'How did X happen?'. The language we have used has dictated our thought - or, perhaps, the communal language that provides us with the word 'Why' itself grows out of our common assumptions. (A question for the linguists: if such questions can be asked in all languages, does this imply a common philosophical assumption about the governance of the universe?)

In the course of centuries of attempts by theologians to establish through logical argument God's existence and attributes (and the inner workings of the Trinity) the Creeds were established as the tests of orthodoxy: see Appendix 4. By the late Middle Ages the emphasis was on the exercise of authority rather than theological speculation: what one was to believe depended on the teaching of the Church, which controlled both theological and scientific learning. Not for nothing was the Bishop of Lincoln the Visitor who supervised Oxford University (then in his large diocese): and the most ancient university, Bologna, was a shining secular, municipal, exception. But even Kant, no Catholic, wrote centuries later 'I had to remove knowledge to make way for faith'.

The concept of Trinity

The Christian God has many aspects; most churches point to a trinity of 'Persons' in one person (or in one 'substance', in medieval philosophy). *The Oxford Dictionary of the Christian Church* (1985 reprint, 575; see also 1394) gives this formal statement: 'the Father ... the Source of all existence, the Son the Eternal Object of the Father's love

24

and the Mediator of that love in creation and redemption, and the Holy Ghost (the Spirit of God) the Bond of Union between Father and Son'. The classical doctrine of the Trinity, that One God exists in Three Persons and One Substance, only dates from the late fourth century; it is not explicit in Scripture. It is a doctrine that puzzles other monotheistic believers - Jews and Muslims - and is declined by Unitarian Christians.

The accessibility of God

The Jew of the Old Testament and today, and the Jewish Christian of the New Testament, worshipped the Father: but perceptions of his nature changed with successive experiences and prophesies. I have mentioned the change from tribal to universal God, and a different attitude towards material benefits. And there was a change in accessibility: the God of Exodus (chs. 19-20) ordered that the priest and people were not to come up Mount Sinai into his presence, 'lest he break forth upon them'. Through Moses he gave the Commandments (once familiar to all in this country) as instructions for personal conduct; the children of Israel were to have no other gods, 'for I ... am a jealous God, visiting the iniquities of the fathers upon the children unto the third and fourth generation of them that hate me ... and showing mercy unto thousands of them that love me, and keep my commandments'. Some 800 pages later in my Bible, and several centuries later in the story Hosea, ch. 6, prophesies that 'thy judgments are as the light that goeth forth. For I desired mercy, and not sacrifice; and the knowledge of God more than burnt offerings. But they like men have transgressed the covenant': the priests have abused the religious processes. Amos, too, gives a stern warning against a lack of integrity in worship, which we as singers should note: 'I hate, I despise your feast days, and I will not smell in your solemn assemblies. Though ye offer me burnt sacrifices and your meat offerings, I will not accept them ... . Take thou away from me the noise of thy songs; for I will not hear the melody of thy viols.'

But from New Testament times followers of Christ (meaning the Anointed One, the Messiah, still originally conceived of as a national saviour) have worshipped God the Father 'through Jesus Christ our Lord'. God has now been seen and experienced in a new and personal way; and Christ is our Advocate with the Father. After a few centuries the mother of Christ, the Blessed Virgin Mary, came to be venerated and regarded as the channel through whom Christ might be influenced in the suppliant's favour. Other saints might also be appealed to, especially if the saint was good at, for example, some form of healing, or protection on a journey. A person named after a saint, or whose church was so dedicated, might first call on that saint for support, and to convey prayers to Christ. And only in Protestant terms was the worshipper allowed to approach God except through the priesthood of the Church: the 'priesthood of all believers', like the provision or reading of the Bible in one's own language, was a grossly offensive idea.

Divine and human Love

The love and loyalty of a devout Christian towards Christ, through whatever channel, is intense and personal. It may be seen as a pale reflection of God's own love for his people, Gentile or Jew; in us it is the emotional strength of Christianity. Through the living presence of Christ (however we understand this) and the workings of the

Holy Spirit of God, this closeness to Christ inspires the Christian's love for his or her fellow-people, inside and outside the Church. George Fox the Quaker, in prison in 1656, wrote that, given this, 'you will come to walk cheerfully over the world, answering *that of God in every one*'. This has great practical significance; love and loyalty can survive persecution to a degree that most of us must find incredible.

One God in diversity?

So the worshipper's response to God has changed over time: one may indeed ask whether the object of worship has not changed - has there been a series of graven images? The normally accepted theory is that we have seen different aspects of the one, unchanging, God. The colour and mode of the response has varied by time, by place and by shade of churchmanship: think now of the differences between Catholic and Orthodox services (or, in musical terms, between Palestrina, Byrd and Mozart on the one hand and Eastern chant and recent works by Arvo Pärt and John Tavener on the other), and contrast Presbyterian psalm-singing with the activities of born-again evangelicals.

Perhaps also (I put myself in the lionesses' jaws) women and men have tended to respond differently. How could they not, when traditionally their lives and upbringings have been so different? The Church has fed these differences with images: the Church is the bride of Christ (remember 'Sleepers, wake'). Women worshippers have sometimes felt a close emotional tie with the male Christ, and the Church's encouragement of the cult of Mary provided a female figure to whom women and men surely reacted differently. Adoration of Mary was at its peak at the same time as the secular (but aristocratic) cult of courtly love (see p. 5) with the desired but inaccessible Queen whose emblem was a rose without a thorn, *rosa sine spinis*. The language here was discretion itself compared with the directness of some Marian texts (*cujus viscera meruerunt portare Dominum* etc.: 'whose entrails [womb] were worthy to bear the Lord'). But the music was, except in convents, in the hands of male singers (as well as composers). A modern mixed choir wishing to sing wholeheartedly medieval and renaissance Catholic music, or even Bach's works for the Thomaskirche, might ponder whether there are hidden tensions to be dealt with.

One truth?

Most Christian Churches have strongly maintained that truth and salvation can only come through Christ (often only through their own Church): hence centuries of attempted conversion, intolerant religious orthodoxy, and religious war. To many of us it is not clear that this was the Founder's intention for his Church: but we have to step back to a pre-Enlightenment outlook if we are to imagine what our inherited religious music is about. Chapters 4 and 6 offer an account of the Catholic and Protestant religions in which, and for which, the music was brought to life.

4. THE CONTEXT OF MEDIEVAL CHURCH MUSIC

At the time of the Reformations of the sixteenth century people throughout western Europe had lived for over a thousand years in an entirely Catholic culture, in which religious ideas and disciplines were pressing and pervasive in a way that is foreign to most modern English minds. We may catch echoes of the earlier world if we witness worship in some Roman Catholic countries, even after the great changes in that Church in the last thirty years. In this chapter I will try to give some idea of the religious outlook of people for whose services late medieval music was written: I concentrate on this period because its music is important to modern singers, and we do have a good amount of historical material, particularly about England and the Low Countries. I have drawn extensively and gratefully on three books: Eamon Duffy, *The Stripping of the Altars*; Margaret Aston, *Faith and Fire*; and Keith Thomas, *Religion and the Decline of Magic*. The musical scene is perhaps best sampled in: Frank Ll. Harrison, *Music in Medieval Britain*; Nicholas Temperley, *The Music of the English Parish Church*; and Reinhard Strohm, *Music in Late Medieval Bruges*.

I deliberately refrain from justifying my statements by footnotes: this is not that sort of book. But do refer to, or even read, these books; they are fascinating as well as lucid.

Belief and worship

'Religion' is a portmanteau word for people's beliefs, hopes, fears, and prayers, and the observance of the services, timetables and ceremonies of the Church's year. All this was important, as now it largely is not, to the individual (even if he revolted against it) and to the community - the parish, or the monastery or convent. The centre of local activity, and the communal symbol, was the church building; and priests, abbots and abbesses were figures of authority, and sometimes great power.

By looking at a few of the thousands of surviving pre-Reformation churches in the British Isles and in western countries of the continent we can grasp the physical and social dominance of the church building, and its various styles and functions. The Gothic style emerged out of the romanesque Norman with pointed arches and vaulting, stone tracery and sharp-cut ornamentation, and often wood carving; and all this gave different acoustics from an early plain Italian basilica or a later German baroque church. In fifteenth-century England the munificence of kings and wealthy citizens, especially wool merchants, allowed the building of the great Perpendicular collegiate churches and chapels, not only in universities but at Windsor Castle, Eton (with its own Choirbook, from around 1500), Tattershall (where Taverner was in charge of music) and St Mary's, Warwick, with its song school. It was in these places and in cathedrals that the grandest music was heard, since this needed not only space but a body of skilled singers. Each building had its own acoustical problems and opportunities.

If we allow for the loss of colour and ornament in later generations, we can imagine the earlier appearance and atmosphere in churches we know - a small country church in England, or a big town church in England or Flanders, in a French cathedral or one of many in England in that style, or in one of the enormous abbey churches like Rievaulx that stand in ruins all over France and the British Isles.

Most of the church services were quite plain, spoken or with sung chant. But where there were the resources, the major feasts of the church's year and saints' days were occasions for a long, brilliant and popular show; there was special enthusiasm for the Virgin Mary and for local patron saints. The church was crowded with standing people; all round were pictures, in stained glass and in the wall-paintings, all with their didactic messages. The liturgy of a High Mass (see pp. 166f) involved far more than words and music - the prescribed ceremonial movements and priestly dress (with their own symbolic meanings), the candles, and in the air the scent of burning incense and the white mist, faintly obscuring the sanctuary round the high altar. The choir sang, in Latin, and out of sight. Though organs were not yet very common, a small choir organ might provide some interludes of polyphony and might accompany chant; in processions chant was supported by the great organ and perhaps by instruments. At the climax of Matins, towards the end of the *Te Deum*, the tower bells (less well tuned before change-ringing began, in the sixteenth century) broke into a 'classicum', the word for a peal of guns, which may suggest the general style: probably a clash of bells.

Much of the service took place in the chancel, behind the screen holding the large rood (the crucifix with the figure of Christ); beyond the chancel, at the east end of the church, was the High Altar. The nave (so called because its vaulted roof looked like an inverted ship, *navis*) was where the townspeople stood; at the end of festal services they joined with the clergy and choir in procession around the inside of the church, and sometimes the churchyard and the streets nearby.

From early medieval times on certain occasions, particularly Good Friday and Easter, the priests sang the Gospel as a simple drama, impersonating the characters. In the later Middle Ages gilds (or 'guilds') staged plays in the streets, as at York, Wakefield, Lincoln and Coventry. These portrayed stages of the Christian story, mixed with local tradition and wit. A 16th-century (Protestant) account of earlier customs in Oxfordshire relates that

In the Dayes of ceremonial Religion they used at *Wytney* to set foorthe yearly in maner of a Shew, or Enterlude, the Resurrection of our Lord and Saviour *Chryste*, partly of Purpose to draw thyther some Concourse of People that might spend their Money in the Towne, but cheiflie to allure by pleasant Spectacle the comon Sort to the Likinge of Popishe Maumetrie; for the which Purpose, and the more lyvely thearby to exhibit to the Eye the hole Action of the Resurrection, the Preistes garnished out certain smalle Puppets, representinge the Parsons of Christe, the Watchmen, *Marie*, and others, amongest the which one bare the Parte of a wakinge Watchman, who (espiinge *Christ* to arise) made a continual Noyce, like to the Sound that is caused by the Metinge of two Styckes, and was therof comonly called, *Jack Snacker of Wytney*.

W. Lamberde, in K. Young, *The Drama of the Medieval Church*, Oxford, 1933, ii, 542f.

('Maumetrie' meant Mohammedanism, or heathenism, associated - wrongly - with the worship of images.)

Inside the church there were wall-paintings, of which a number survive in England and France. A favourite subject (surviving in Hornton, Oxon.) was the Doom, or Last Judgment, with Christ at the centre of the redeemed souls, rising on our left to Heaven, and the unrepentant in

32

torment at the bottom right corner. What happened after death was a central pre-occupation, to which I return later. The glass of the windows, especially in well-endowed churches, showed prophets, kings and saints and biblical scenes from which the priest could instruct his flock - Church and King forbade possession of a vernacular Bible even when the translation had been achieved and printing had made wide diffusion possible. Images in stone or wood were increasingly displayed. Adornment and maintenance in the chancel tended to be the responsibility of the priest; the nave was looked after by the people - especially rich donors concerned for their souls - and the town gilds. This duty was sometimes fulfilled on the grand scale, as we see from elaborate chapels and chantries in big churches, and from family tombs inscribed with requests for prayers by the whole community which the donor had left behind.

Outside there might be stone carvings of saints, angels, and musicians with their instruments, or of men who built the church; on the north, the Devil's side, the gargoyles and friezes could be grotesque and frightening, perhaps embodying pagan memories. All around in the churchyard were the graves of parishioners (without much of the massive stonework fashionable later); the ground itself was holy through consecration with salt and water (so a person excommunicated or a suicide had to be buried at a distance). After the expected Second Coming of Christ there would be a 'general resurrection' when the graves would be opened for the Last Judgment and the dead would come to life, as imagined in Stanley Spencer's painting in the Tate Gallery *The Resurrection: Cookham*.

The community and its timetable

The unit of local community, especially outside the boroughs, was the parish. This was both civil and ecclesiastical. It was a small part of the county, in which the sheriff (shire-reeve) represented the King's interests in administration and justice; people were also subject to the remaining feudal courts, to the judges administering the common law, and to Papal canon law in the bishop's ecclesiastical court. Within the parish the church was the centre of government; the vicar and churchwardens were powers in the land until, indeed, quite recently. An abbey, like Abingdon or Reading, would own much of the town around it, and the abbot ruled: indeed, when Henry VIII dissolved the monasteries, local government disappeared and it had to be improvised by local people or gilds.

The religious supervision of the vicar and his parish lay with the bishop, appointed by the Pope. A monastic institution such as an abbey was outside the bishop's realm, and was responsible to the head of the monastic Order to which it belonged, often on the Continent, and thence to the Pope. Since the Norman conquest the King had had great influence in appointing both bishops and abbots: but these overseas allegiances were all terminated when Henry VIII both assumed the earthly headship of the English Church and dissolved the monasteries.

Outside these two hierarchies were the friars, of various Orders, who wandered round teaching; many of the more didactic medieval carols are likely to be their work - for instance, 'There is no rose', p. 4 above.

Medieval England had fifty feast days on which all but the most essential agricultural work was forbidden. There was a duty to fast on the eve of such days and to attend Mass, Matins and Evensong on the day. Sometimes a feast day would grow out of pagan observances, from pre-Christian times, which the Church authorities knew were popular but difficult to snuff out. One such was Rogation, when evil spirits who created division between neighbours and sickness in man and beast were (it was believed) driven away. Rogationtide emphasised the parish community (alive and departed), and the boundaries dividing it from others, so the celebrations included processions around the parish bounds, sometimes with handbells (to banish demons) and banners. The litany of the saints was sung, and at a number of crosses on the boundary the vicar read from the gospel, and prayers were offered for good weather and fertility. When the procession returned, the good communal spirit was further encouraged by ale, food and bonfires. (It is intriguing, if irrelevant, that Rogation observance was started by a fifth-century French bishop whose diocese - *ODCC*, 1193, tells us - had been troubled by volcanic eruptions.) We can see the closeness of this religion to magic conjurings, lasting through from pre-Christian times; communal activities were also a primitive and ancient form of group-therapy.

Another great feast, this time Christian in origin, was Corpus Christi (still a great public event in Catholic Europe), when the Host, the consecrated bread transformed into the Body of Christ, was borne aloft for all to see and venerate. This only began in England in 1318, but it quickly became a popular and civic event when householders decorated the streets, and the trade and charitable gilds might mount their devotional 'mystery plays'. The ceremony echoed the moment in the Eucharistic Mass when the priest elevated the Host at the moment of its consecration, saying *Hoc est enim Corpus Meum* ('For truly this is My Body'), and the *Sanctus* bell was rung so that the people knew they should look up from their private devotions. The motet for Corpus Christi was *Ave verum corpus* - here they could actually see the true body, miraculously transformed from bread. They asked for mercy (*miserere mei*) as they contemplated the pierced side and the gushing blood of Christ, son of Mary, praying that they should taste him before their death. The words are intense and committed; with this in mind we can perhaps feel the great force in Byrd's setting (post-medieval but highly traditional in belief), and we may hesitate before throwing it into a programme on the grounds that it's in only four parts and we've sung it before.

In the absence of radio and newspapers the medieval community relied on the church to show people where they were in the year, through its yearly timetable. The Church's year (see Appendix 1) starts with Advent, which includes the four Sundays before Christmas. Certain dates, notably Christmas, Epiphany and Candlemas, were related to the civil (solar) calendar, and the dates were the same each year. Others depended on the moon, as does the Jewish Passover, and varied with Easter (which is, in the Western Church, the first Sunday after the first full moon on or after 21 March). Ash Wednesday, the beginning of Lent, is forty days earlier (not counting Sundays); Ascension Day, a Thursday, is forty days later (counting Sundays); Whitsun, like the Jewish Feast of Weeks (in Greek, 'Pentecost'), is fifty days inclusive, or seven weeks, after Easter (note the ancient and persisting fascination with holy or magic numbers); Trinity Sunday is a week later, and Corpus Christi on the following Thursday. Rogationtide was the Sunday to Wednesday before Ascension Day, and thus, like Corpus Christi, a summer occasion (though the 'Major Rogation' fell on the fixed date of 25 April). Working life as well as worship depended on these dates: so when printing started (in the second half of the fifteenth century), books or pamphlets containing calendars were best-sellers. Liturgical and astrological dates were combined, as in an almanac, and often included in a 'primer', which aimed to provide the quite numerous literate laity with prayers and religious instruction. For most people religion was a ritual method of living rather than a system of belief.

Heaven, Hell, and Purgatory

In reading about religious life at this time one is struck by the prominent part taken by thought about death. Given the uncertainty of life because of disease, fire and other accident, and sometimes war and famine, this is understandable. But there was more to it than that. We have largely lost - been emancipated from? - the pressing fear of what happens to one thereafter. And when our texts ask for mercy (*Kyrie eleison, Christe eleison; miserere nobis; peccatorum miserere*) we may not feel urgency, because (mostly) we do not have the same fear of Hell or of Purgatory, nor see earthly misfortunes as being caused by the Devil, requiring divine relief. Death must mean losses, whatever one's expectation about joys in Heaven; the person is lost to family and community; one's own valued life on earth ceases; abilities and stored experience are switched off like work in progress on a computer.

But can even the non-believer be sure of nothingness? Hamlet, soliloquising in Act III, i - and I give the words of his argument without the seductive beauty of the verse - would be glad not to 'bear the whips and scorns of time, the oppressor's wrong, the proud man's contumely, the pangs of dispriz'd love' (etc.) and instead 'to die: to sleep'. But 'in that sleep of death what dreams may come'? The 'dread of something after death ... puzzles the will, and makes us rather bear those ills we have than fly to others that we know not of'. And in *Measure for Measure* (III, i) Claudio, condemned to death, but anxious to live at all costs (even at the cost of his sister Isabella's virginity), speaks of the terrors of death: not only physical decay and hell-fire but the endless nothingness of the spirit 'imprison'd in the viewless winds and blown with restless violence round about the pendant world'. Hamlet was a prince and an intelligent man, and Shakespeare was writing for an audience that was used to Renaissance thought: but medieval fears were still all too familiar.

...

I must now attempt a statement of what was believed in medieval Catholicism, both official and popular; some of this is very strange to modern minds.

Sin, and punishment after death

Horror and fear are the emotions most commonly associated with late medieval perceptions of death and the life everlasting, and 'preachers, dramatists and moralists did not hesitate to employ terror ... to stir their audiences to penitence and good works' (Duffy, 313f). Caxton's translation of *The Mirrour of the World* (1480) describes 'a pitte of fyre ... ful of alle stenche and of sorowes, anguysshes, heuynes [heavings], hungre and thyrste'. This might not be the view of sophisticated theologians, but it was a great help to the Church and secular powers in maintaining earthly discipline. Preachers through the ages have kept quiet about what had been admitted in the early third century AD - that heaven and hell are only relevant for the motivation of very inferior capacities (Clement of Alexandria), and that Biblical language about punishment by everlasting fire - to intelligent Christians, Origen says, an expression of God's remedial and purifying processes - was justified because many can only be deterred by fear from leading a sinful life (H. Chadwick, *Early Christian Thought and the Classical Tradition*, 42, 78).

Throughout life there was emphasis on one's sinfulness. Theologians from the early centuries onwards developed St Paul's doctrine (Romans 5, 12-21), emphasising that Adam's original sin was transmitted to all through the act of conjugal generation (there were disagreements as to how far this was the fault of sexual concupiscence). So a baby, before it could be in a fit state to be baptised into the church, had to have evil spirits ceremoniously exorcised (and without baptism it could never enter Heaven, remaining in an in-between 'limbo'); and women after childbirth were purified in a 'churching' service before they could again take communion.

After the death of the body the 'Particular Judgment' sent the soul on one of two paths. ('Soul', a difficult concept for many of us, means that which is the continuing element in a human life, is capable of consciousness, feeling and willing.) In the absence of confession and repentance of sins, and absolution by a priest, the soul would be sent to the torments of Hell, permanently beyond the reach of love and of prayer, with punishments matched to its sins. (Thus all outside the Catholic Church were deemed to be so condemned - one reason for later disputes about the legitimacy of the Anglican priesthood, as well as one cause of strife with Jews and Muslims.)

The doctrine, which settled down in 1274, was that if there had been confession, repentance and forgiveness, the soul would go to Purgatory for a considerable period, where the torments were like those in Hell. (St Thomas

Aquinas had taught that the smallest pain in Purgatory was greater than the greatest on earth, though he added - as late medieval English Catholics did not - that the certitude of salvation would give deep peace amid the pain.) But from Christ's sacrifice there derived a 'treasury of merits', which could be unlocked and spent on behalf of suffering souls. Part of the debt to God still remained; this had to be worked off by one's good deeds and by the prayers of other faithful people. Only then would the holy soul - not yet with its spiritual body - be led by angels to Heaven in deep peace for eternity: *Justorum animae in manu Dei sunt, et non tanget illos tormentum mortis* - the souls of the righteous are in the hand of God, and no torment of death touches them). In Heaven the blessed would see God, the Divine Being, and indeed see all that they had reasonable interest in knowing. (Theologians may have had in mind the forbidden tree of knowledge of good and evil.) Souls entirely without sin - and this could only have been some of the saints - would miss Purgatory and go directly to Heaven after death.

This 'Particular Judgment', coming immediately the soul separates from the body at death, was a theological construct which faced the fact that the imminent Second Coming of Christ, the *Parousia*, was obviously being deferred. At that point the present world was to end, the dead would rise from the grave ('Messiah', 'The trumpet shall sound'), their souls would be brought from Hell, Purgatory or Heaven. They would join the living for the Last (or 'General') Judgment. Those granted salvation would go to their heavenly life, with a spiritual body, entering fully into bliss with the whole company of Heaven, including their dear ones. The rest would go to Hell. After the shattering fall of Rome in 410 (to a Christian but heretical Visigoth) St Augustine reassessed Christian doctrine, suggesting that the soul did not have to wait indefinitely for bliss or damnation, but that there would be a Particular Judgment (pp. 39f) immediately after death. It seems that those alive at the Last Day would be dealt with in the Last Judgment, but this area remained confused.

The worshipper was deeply conscious that after death he would be sent to Purgatory or to Hell. So he was concerned both with avoiding Hell and with earning remission of the length of his own sentence in Purgatory by good works and gifts to the church and to charity: and he wanted to reduce the time that the souls of his family and community already in Purgatory would spend there. A system of 'indulgences' grew up, depending on papal authority (and was massively abused until the sale of indulgences was prohibited in the reforms of the sixteenth century). If a state of grace had been achieved (through repentance, confession and absolution), acts such as pilgrimage or the recitation of certain devotions could earn forty days' remission, or some other period. Occasionally total remission could be granted if a special relic were displayed, or a Jubilee declared at Rome. Extraordinary beliefs grew up: the Fifteen Oes were prayers on Christ's passion, each starting 'O Jesus', written by St Bridget of Sweden after a vision of Christ; if one recited these prayers, the souls of fifteen of one's kindred could be released from Purgatory. These were among the popular devotions published in Latin Books of Hours and vernacular Primers.

Gifts to the Church (perhaps for the rebuilding of St Peter's, Rome, or for one's parish church) earned remission: or a rich man might found a college or a hospital. The very rich bought multiple masses and indulgences; Cardinal Albrecht of Bavaria amassed 39 million years of remission, and Henry VIII ordered daily masses for as long as the world should endure (Aston, 15). Margery Kempe of King's Lynn assembled and wrote about a multitude of indulgences; she was granted those attached to the Holy Places in Jerusalem without going there - and even, enterprisingly, granted these to others.

Despite complaints about abuses, the indulgence system deeply affected churchgoers of all stations in life. Their words and actions do suggest a literal belief in torments after death, in the need for mercy and in the efficacy of prayers and good deeds to reduce these sufferings. When they sang or heard *Kyrie eleison* it was surely heartfelt, and not just the piece that began the Ordinary of the Mass. Likewise when they gave generously they were hoping for real relief in Purgatory as well as wanting to help Church finances, buildings and charities, which benefited greatly in late medieval times.

These riches enhanced the status and power of the clergy, which was underpinned by their flock's fear of Hell, where there was no remission and no end. People could only escape Hell if their sins had been confessed and absolved, and this required the services of a priest. Before any Christian died, the Devil's evil spirits were expected to make a last attempt to capture his soul, and the priest's ministrations at the deathbed tried to wrest the soul from these attacks and to persuade the dying person to repent - to turn to Christ and accept his mercy. Many priests showed particularly close and sympathetic concern for their parishioners at the deathbed; and the earliest prayers published in English (Duffy, 320f) are similarly concerned with pleas to Christ for preservation and for the Lord God's forgiveness in the face of death.

The regular services in church were well attended, perhaps especially when the priest was sympathetic and conscientious. People were indeed conscious that death was inevitable and might be early, and that salvation and the reduction of torment after death needed the offices of the Church. Weekday masses focused private devotion for those who chose to attend: but going to Sunday Mass was part of living in a local community, and was expected by one's fellows as well as the law of the land. The coherence of the Church and the local community meant that, despite great inequalities and hardships, rather high degrees of social order and discipline were usually maintained. The Church was the keystone; its position (and wealth) gave enormous power.

The Blessed Virgin Mary, and other saints

The cult of the saints cast a 'poetic enchantment' over medieval Europe (Emile Mâle: Duffy, 155); we have seen (p. 34-7) how this affected the calendar not only of worship but of work and feasting. This became more intense in the couple of centuries before the sixteenth-century Reformations, and Marianism was its most striking aspect.

In Catholic doctrine the Blessed Virgin Mary is the saint most to be venerated (not worshipped: that belongs to God only). She was the human vehicle in whom the Holy Spirit conceived God's Word, his only Son, Jesus, born in lowliness to live among us and to will his own death as a sacrifice sufficient to redeem the sins of all who believe in Him. She was loved intensely as the perfect woman (whereas the three aspects of Deity were thought of as male); she was mother, advocate and guardian. She was *Stella maris*, Star of the Sea, and her prayers were therefore effective against shipwreck. And for the educated and poetic there was a strong echo of the unattainable Lady of the tradition of courtly love (see p. 5).

A vast amount of poetry and music was addressed to Mary, often of high quality. Where a large musical establishment had been endowed, votive motets or antiphons addressed to Mary could be on a grand scale, as the Eton Choirbook shows. Nevertheless this singing (perhaps, as at Eton, before an image of the Virgin) was a personal and corporate devotion for those in the enclosed space of the chapel or chancel; it was, Frank Harrison says (219), the universal and characteristic expression of the devotional fervour of the later Middle Ages. However, on special days such as the Purification (Presentation in the Temple, or Candlemas, 2 February), a large-scale antiphon might be sung to the whole congregation from the steps of the chancel at the conclusion of Mass.

At the Annunciation the archangel Gabriel told Mary that she was to be the mother of the Saviour. Mary then visited her 'cousin' Elizabeth, who had just conceived John the Baptist, and spoke the words of *Magnificat* (Luke 1); after votive antiphons, this is the most frequently set text in late medieval England. The mystery of the lowliness of the birth is explored in *O magnum mysterium* (Byrd, G. Gabrieli, Palestrina, Poulenc, Victoria), in which the Mother is addressed as *Beata Virgo* and *Ave Maria*. Medieval carols show the popularity of simple and didactic poems about Mary - 'There is no rose', and 'Hail Mary, full of grace'.

Through Mary, fount of grace, the devout could easily approach Christ. She was especially important as the Lady of Mercy, and thus the saint of the deathbed. This may explain why so many wealthy people sought to ease their passages to Heaven by endowing chantries or chapels in her name. But besides the wish for a holy death comforted by the sacraments, and eventual salvation, people looked to religion in late medieval times for moderate prosperity, safety from enemies, and healing from disease. For divine intervention in these worldly matters they invoked the help of a number of other saints. St Roche and St Sebastian were good at the plague; St Margaret or the Virgin Mary might reduce the pangs of labour. A popular saint was King Henry VI (founder of King's College, Cambridge, and Eton College); so was Thomas à Becket from the time of his martyrdom (see *Music in honour of St Thomas of Canterbury*, ed. D. Stevens, Novello, 1970).

Generally the saints were seen as gentle, loving and merciful, like Jesus himself: but saints could do unfriendly acts. William Tyndale derisively asks 'Who is not afraid of St Laurence? Who dare deny St Anthony a fleece of wool for fear of his terrible fire, or lest he send the pox among our sheep?' Popular credulity was such that the coals on which Laurence was toasted (in Rome, in the legend) were believed to have been discovered at Bury St Edmunds. There were many bizarre beliefs about the powers of individual saints. We may not meet them often in the surviving music, but if a saint's name is mentioned the singer may understand the text better after looking up the saint's particular function: one can refer to the indexes to Aston, Duffy and Thomas, to dictionaries of saints, and to details in Thomas, page 38, n. 8.

Popular piety might go further than orthodox doctrine, and trust in magic was often not far away. This is not surprising, given that missionaries in, for instance, Anglo-Saxon England had built up the saints' miraculous powers in order to persuade people out of paganism. Images of saints - sculptures or paintings - were sanctioned by Pope Gregory (c.600 AD) as laymen's books, imagery for the illiterate. Veneration of saints might be extended to their images; if unsophisticated pilgrims had undergone a hard journey to a shrine they expected to be able to 'see' their saint. This helps to explain people's tenacious defence of statues and pictures, and the motives of reformers who wanted images removed and destroyed.

The literate could buy popular lives of the saints as early as the twelfth century; and even up to the Reformation the Church countenanced optimistic prayers for supernatural cures and reliefs from physical dangers, and allowed or encouraged images, relics, shrines and pilgrimages. The cult of the saints was firmly embraced by the laity of all classes. Duffy (186) suggests that it gave assurance of the possibility of rescue from the iron laws of cause and effect in a harsh life.

Devotion to the Holy Name of Jesus was popularised by the Franciscans in the fifteenth century: hence the hymns *O bone Jesu* and *Jesu dulcis memoria*. (It recurs, quoting Philippians 2, 10-11, in the Victorian hymn *At the name of Jesus every knee shall bow*.) In England the feast day is 7 August. Meditation on the Passion became a central devotional activity.

In the late Middle Ages there was a widespread growth of private devotion, using Books of Hours or 'Primers'; these were not just for highly educated readers, and printing allowed the sale of quite large numbers. The Rosary was an old-established system of devotion; a string of beads was counted to keep count of its Fifteen Mysteries, divided into three Chaplets (the Joyful, Sorrowful and Glorious Mysteries of the lives of Mary and Jesus); each Chaplet had five Decades, each of which consisted of the Paternoster or Lord's Prayer, ten Hail Marys, and the *Gloria Patri*.

In this atmosphere the cults of Mary, the saints and the Name of Jesus, and the Passion (with the Five Wounds and the Seven Words), combine in what Duffy (447) calls 'the lush affectivity of medieval piety' - a popular aspect of medieval Catholicism that evoked a very strong reaction from Protestant reformers of the 1520s and 1530s.

Magic and miracle

Official Church leaders were sometimes wary of popular enthusiasm for the invocation of saints and their relics, images and legends, and for the prodigious physical results expected from Divine power. A manual of 1489 says that all who write or believe promises of relief against disaster or cure of sickness sin grievously - though it adds 'But yf they be symple people and so ignoraunt of symplesse / that by ignoraunce they be excused' (Duffy, 277). And remarkable supernatural reliefs promised in an alleged 'letter to Charlemagne', and included in English *Horae* (Books of Hours), were not allowed to be included in French *Horae* (Duffy, 273-9).

It was not just folk-religion however that saw humanity as beleaguered by hostile troops of devils, and aimed to exorcise them. The Church's liturgies for Rogationtide and baptism involved words and symbols whose use in any secular ceremonies would be called witchcraft or magic - which was severely punished in ecclesiastical courts as well as in the Assizes. The use of candles, holy water and salt was approved for protection against evils and disasters, whether in the church or at home.

Natural disasters were often the devil's work, but they could also be an Act of God, a phrase then taken more literally than today. The great early reformer John Wycliffe blamed the 1382 earthquake on recent decisions about heresy taken by the Church's Blackfriars Council; and such interpretations of God's 'providence' long survived the Reformation.

In this, Wycliffe presumably did not regard himself as superstitious: he was a critical man. He was indeed condemned for denying the Church's teaching about transubstantiation. There is a miracle at the centre of the Mass; when the bread and wine are consecrated, Catholic doctrine was, and is, that their substance changes and that they become the Body and Blood of Christ in a real and not merely symbolic sense. Catholic authorities were insistent on this point; the genuineness of the miracle strengthened their central authority, for it was under this that the priest performed the Mass. The Church's teachings and liturgical traditions were seen to be effective and valid.

Wycliffe considered that the sacrament of the altar had become a mystery of the wrong kind (Aston, 55, 60); what we should worship is not a sign but what the sign represents. The popular attachment to images was so strong that zealots among the reformers later reacted with violent and systematic destruction inside the churches.

We may note that the modern form of the Mass, Catholic and Anglican, includes the phrase 'may be *to us* his body and his blood'. The doctrinal chasm is papered over by skilled drafting so that it is possible to partake while holding Wycliffe's view, or the opposite.

The distinction between magic and miracles and, indeed, the sacramental mysteries, was a fine one, and it troubled theologians for centuries. For secular magic, the Church made distinctions according to the nature of the magician's intention, or according to the magic's effect; the possible severity of the punishments meant that this was not an academic point (Duffy, 73, 279-82). The ability to call on supernatural channels was valued by the recipients: it gave them power. Thomas (291f) quotes estimates made around 1500 that there were as many wizards (cunning-men, conjurers) as there were parochial clergy: the Church courts might take action against their use of charms or divination. Later, when in England and Scotland what could be regarded as Popish magic was banned, the popular need persisted; Thomas, 298-300, quotes the Aldeburgh churchwardens reporting of a 'wise woman' in 1597 that 'She taketh upon her to cure diseases by prayer, and therefore hath recourse of people to her far and wide'. In some parts there were long and tragic battles against witchcraft through the following centuries.

Indeed, pre-Christian practices and ways of thinking were deeply embedded, especially in the countryside; the Church absorbed some, knowing that it needed popular support and that it was easier to adapt old customs than to wipe them out. In the ancient Celtic Beltane fires and human sacrifices of 1 May there may have had a pre-Christian symbolism of death and rebirth; this and the Saxon spring festival of Eustre are probably the remote ancestors of traditional rural May Day goings-on.

In its early days the Church made two pagan festivals into major Christian feasts: the turn of the winter, Yule, the greatest festival of the Church. So joy in the miracles of birth and rebirth breaks into the familiar sombreness of suffering and death; and each year the joy, if we will have it, is born again.

5. THE POWER OF WORDS

WORDS IN RITUAL

In the medieval Catholicism which I have been discussing, the recitation of certain prayers was believed in itself to give various reliefs, whether in this life or in Purgatory. Some of these prayers were accepted by Church authorities as orthodox Catholic practice, and they often sprang from genuine piety (Thomas, 588; Duffy, 269-79). Others had manipulative intent, or were on the outer edge of orthodoxy, like the more extravagant reliefs offered as indulgences. We have seen (pp. 48f) that there were many secular wizards, and their magical conjurations might exploit popular credulity through the use of ecclesiastical phrases.

The use of ritual words could have powerful effects on one's enemy, on the safety of cattle and the fertility of cornfields, and in religious supplication. (This was firmly believed in: indeed, a curse could sometimes actually have fatal effects on another person - at least, if he knew about it.) Religious words of ritual were held by theologians to be effective even if used by wicked men, which is why priests objected to their use in popular magic. Perhaps the most important point for modern singers to realise is the Catholic doctrine that in the celebration of a sacrament, and in particular the Mass, neither the character of the priest nor the comprehension of the congregation is relevant to its effectiveness: the sacrament confers grace *ex opere operato* (from the act that has been done). We shall consider in Chapter 10 what the moral is for those of us who sing Catholic music, liturgically or not, and notice the change in Protestant and Catholic attitudes to words at the Reformation.

Belief in the power of words used as ritual is very old. Speaking a name was from very early times believed to give power over the person named (J.G. Frazer, *The Golden Bough*, 244-62). So a Greek priest of the mysteries, or an Egyptian god, might not be spoken of by name lest enemies gain power over him.

The Jews from *c.*300 BC tried to avoid speaking the name of God, then spelt YHWH or JHVH (cf. the modern Jewish usage, 'G-d'). They substituted the Hebrew word for Lord, *Adonai*, which was later taken over in Christian worship as the Greek *Kyrios* and then as Latin *Dominus*. When vowel signs came to be added in Hebrew, instead of 'Yahweh' (probably the original sound), confusingly the vowels from *Adonai* were used, which is how we get *Jehovah*. The original word may have been *Yah*; this perhaps means 'to be', which may lie behind apparently mysterious passages like Exodus 3, 13f: 'What is his name? ... I AM THAT I AM ... I AM hath sent me unto you'.

The Word and the creative imagination

We must note the significance in Judaism and Christianity of 'the Word'. *Logos* also means Reason, and some Greek philosophers used this to denote the force behind the world. In Genesis 1 the light, the firmament, the earth and the seas and the rest of creation were made by God's word - by what God *said*. In the New Testament, in John 1, 'In the beginning was the Word' means the Creative Word, made flesh among us in Jesus - and therefore not created by the Father, as the Arians held. The Word turns up in our singing: being made flesh in *Verbum caro factum est* (e.g. Schütz), and robustly in 'Messiah', 'The Lord gave the Word'.

We are getting into a deep and important area for understanding religious thought - the symbolic language of mystery and myth (in the strict sense of that word), and the accession or infusion to us of creative power. For singers this exploration may begin to elucidate sacred texts which appear unacceptable to our modern minds, and make sense of the words-and-music which, as artists and/or worshippers, we are seeking to re-create.

There is a lively but serious little book by Edward Robinson, *The Language of Mystery*, with useful thoughts on imagination and fantasy. In its preface Bishop John V. Taylor quotes Coleridge's description of the creative *imagination* as 'a repetition in the finite mind of the eternal act of creation in the infinite I AM'. This reminds us of St John's account, which I have just mentioned, of the Creative Word which came to dwell among us, and at Pentecost sent the Holy Spirit of truth (John 14, 17) to be with us after his departure. Perhaps, if we consider acts of self-forgetful creativity, we may see that Spirit working through us, and the mystery of our art as the revelation of something which is 'other' (I avoid the word 'transcendental'). Robinson (25) suggests we see imagination as openness to *grace*, and adds that to put our trust in it is no more and no less than to have *faith* in what it may reveal to us; humanly speaking, faith becomes possible through the means of the imagination. This imagination in depth he calls 'vertical' (12), and he points to the lateral imagination by which we - and that means, in our context, composers and singers - share these vertical insights with our fellow men and women.

Lastly, on the Word, in what way do the words of the Bible carry for us God's authority? For most Christians, except fundamentalists, truth needs to be sought in an understanding and critical manner. Bishop Ian T. Ramsay put this felicitously (*Religious Language*, 151):

Here is the Bible as 'the Word of God'. The Bible is *not* the 'words of God' ... but its words make the light to dawn, make situations come alive, evoke that kind of situation which demand the word 'God'.

Mystery, myth, metaphor

What we call *metaphor* plays a central part in symbolic language; it is a name or descriptive term used, the *SOED* says rather distantly, for 'some object to which it is not properly applicable', and quotes Addison, 'Those beautiful Metaphors in Scriptures, where Life is termed a Pilgrimage'. Janet Martin Soskice, *Metaphor and Religious Language*, 159, points to the OT as 'the source of Christian descriptive language and particularly of metaphors which have embodied a people's understanding of God'.

Some of us, trained scientifically rather than in the ways of literature and poetry, are cautious about statements which do not point to a common-sense reality. We may trace the universe back in time by successive application of scientific laws: but a point comes when the dry land of possible knowledge is touched by an ocean of *mystery*. We can ignore this if we are sufficiently prosaic, or we can try to see whether imaginative concepts or pictures enrich our understanding and arouse some response to this ocean. When science has done all it can, to push further requires us to think in some different mode (or dimension), guided perhaps by imagination or fantasy, or by an established religious or mythological framework: this is where we find the idea of God, or of several gods. The ocean of mystery may become a sea of (perhaps uncritical) faith. ('Mystery' must be used with caution; other meanings include the doctrines and sacramental acts of a Church or sect, and the secrets and skills of a trade.)

Many ancient civilisations were not troubled to distinguish sharply between the dry land of fact and the mysterious sea. They had the talent and taste for story-telling - invaluable, we may imagine, during long winter evenings in the desert. Religious *myth* grew when the story-teller was concerned with wide and deep matters - creation, birth, fertility and growth, power, good and evil, space, time and death. Gods were postulated and sometimes personalised, and men tried to harness their power and assuage their anger, and pass on their thoughts in vivid stories.

The master-craftsman Daedalus made wax wings for himself and his son Icarus so that they could fly out of Crete to escape King Minos. Daedalus got to Sicily safely, but Icarus disobeyed flight instructions, flew too near the sun, and suffered a fatal landing in the sea. There's a moral there somewhere, and it doesn't depend on historical accuracy; and the hearers probably did not try to distinguish fact from fiction as closely as we (sometimes) do. Likewise with the story of Adam, Eve and the serpent in Genesis 3 or that of the Good Samaritan in Luke 10, 25-37, which convincingly answers the question put to Jesus 'And who is my neighbour?'. The value of Shakespeare's insights which he conveys to us through Portia and Shylock, King Lear, or the Macbeths, does not depend on their historical accuracy - nor does their great literary value guarantee such accuracy.

So when we sing *Magnificat* it is not to the point to consider whether St Luke (1, 46-55) correctly recorded what Mary said to Elisabeth; still less whether Mary was right in saying that the Lord had put down the mighty from their seat. We are giving live musical flesh to Mary's song of adoring praise, within Luke's version of the Christian Gospel. (NT scholars have to look much more closely in order to separate history and evangelical doctrine; perhaps Luke deliberately set the non-apocalyptic tone of his Gospel by the serenity of *Magnificat* and the *Benedictus* which follows in vv. 68-79.) We shall come back to these matters, particularly in the chapters on Christmas and Easter music.

False prophets, received truths, and our need to choose

To all these stories the hearer brought his own experience and problems, and so there were differing effects on each hearer's mind and will. A good image or metaphor has a power of vivid suggestion which can appeal in different ways to different temperaments, and this is imaginatively fruitful: Shakespeare starts *Henry V* with

O! for a Muse of fire, that would ascend/ The brightest heaven of invention;
A kingdom for a stage ... .

This richness of association allows a variety of interpretation, which a factual and clear-cut statement purposely avoids. Rhetorical devices such as metaphors can have great persuasive power in the life of the hearer, and a great writer can handle this without dangerous ambiguity: but the rhetoric can add to the danger for simple or susceptible hearers if a charismatic speaker, political or religious, is muddled, deluded, or just plain evil.

We have to be able to distinguish enthusiastic delusion, or falsehood, from the true vine. Mixing the metaphors somewhat, 'Beware of false prophets, which come to you in sheep's clothing, but inwardly they are ravening wolves. Ye shall know them by their fruits. Do men gather grapes of thorns, or figs of thistles?' (Matthew 7, 15f). The fruits are the lives and works of the faithful. However, we have to beware of a possible circularity of argument; any self-respecting religion will be valid when tested by its own principles. We each have our own set of values, which we can apply to those who may be true or false prophets. Can we distinguish the negative, perverting and destructive from that which makes all things new, or purifies in the fire? We can only do this in deep and calm thought after the rhetoric is over, and in the openness to our deepest realities which is prayer.

Is this not mere subjectivism? Yes, although I would omit 'mere'. Each of us has to decide about our life, our preferences and values. But it is important that we should be able (and willing) to communicate this outlook to others who may decide differently; and communication may mature and modify our own outlook, without the temptation to contradict or eliminate what others say and feel. The community of those who accept and follow the outlook of Jesus Christ makes up the Church; some arrive by conscious choice and decision, but perhaps many more are there as 'cradle' members, accepting the judgments of the Church on matters of doctrine and dogma as a matter of loyal submission.

Mystery come to life

Scholars can attempt to sort out historical fact in a religious tradition from the story-telling. But the significance of some central mysteries lies in a different dimension - in their effects on human lives. We have the opportunity today to accept new life through the Eucharist; and in first-century Jerusalem the Resurrection led to a transformation of the lives of the early disciples, from dejected defeat to a sense of victory and purpose.

We can accept this while noting that it does not guarantee truth or sense in every statement that Christians make; nor can we deny misconduct by authorities or members of the organised Church through all too much of its history. The test for us is whether in our lives and our communities the Resurrection mystery will be free to show its creative and transforming power.

How? There is a wonderful book by the late H.A. Williams, *True Resurrection*, written when, with knowledge of the fullness and the pains of life, he had retired as a Cambridge chaplain to a monastic community; I recommend particularly his Chapters 1, 2 and 6. Early in the book he gives vivid examples of how personal love and happiness, artistic creativity, health and vigour may be transformed through an acceptance and openness to new life; in this (160) he sees resurrection, a 'coming to be' which is the creative mystery of all life, the continuing miracle of creation, 'a calling of things that are not into existence. It is the giving of life to what has no life'.

He is interpreting metaphors of Christ's resurrection and the new life of his disciples, pointing to mysteries which we can ignore if we feel entirely fact-bound, and using words, carefully, in a creative - poetic? - mode. But the words can lose their vital spark; orthodox religion, he says (97), processes and packages the mystery in verbalised concepts. These abstract what is real from the realities they set out to describe. This affects the faith of the devout; they become insensitive to reality, and 'deaf to the Eternal Word speaking through all things'. He quotes (100) Auden's dictum that dogmatic theological statements are to be comprehended neither as logical propositions nor as poetic utterances: they are to be taken rather as shaggy-dog stories: they have a point, but he who tries too hard to get it will miss it.

Yes - but we can see how difficult it is for the non-devout to respect ecclesiastical doctrines - and how very much is lost because it is difficult to grasp the intent of ancient ways of thinking. This chapter can only say 'there are minefields'; Harry Williams will take the reader further, and I shall come back to him in my last chapter.

The combination of sung music with words which, when used liturgically, are already potent has long been held to add emotional and persuasive force: but its beauty or complexity may distract. We must tread carefully here, and consider when our music was written; in the humanist Renaissance, followed by the Protestant and Catholic Reformations, composers began to seek musical means to intensify, not dissipate, the message in the text. I pursue this in Chapter 10.

In commenting on the way people expressed their beliefs in pre-Reformation Europe, I have tried to see how far modern singers can empathise with, or even surrender willingly to, the meaning of the words. My attempts at elucidation claim no Catholic authority, but I have tried not to risk offence and to be constructive. If my outlook is felt to be Protestant, liberal and non-conformist I cannot object.

We turn now to the world after the Reformation.

6. AFTER THE REFORMATION

Over the centuries the Catholic Church had developed faults so great that reforming action was needed. This took two forms: the Protestant Reformation, with a separation from the control of the Pope, and the Counter-Reformation within the Roman Catholic Church itself. The Church had for centuries been immensely powerful and also wealthy; in late medieval times its wealth, and often that of well-placed individuals, grew through the granting of indulgences in return for donations by the faithful. We have seen how fears of Hell or long endurance of Purgatory influenced donors, and some ways in which the Church communities and its priests benefited: but gross abuse developed, especially in the activities of professional sellers of papal pardons, real or purported. In about 1387 Chaucer's Pardoner tells us how he exploits credulous congregations for his own profit (*Canterbury Tales*, 'The Prologue to the Pardoner's Tale'). There was wide revulsion in German churches when Pope Julius II offered indulgences for contributions to the rebuilding of St Peter's, Rome, and a Dominican friar preached that as soon as the coin rang in the chest, the soul for whom money had been paid would go straight to Heaven (avoiding the painful and inconvenient stage of Purgatory).

Protestantism; Luther and Calvin

The various groups which became known as Protestants, from Wycliffe and others in the fourteenth century, spoke out against abuse: but also they were concerned with deeper matters - the source of the Church's authority, and the need to maintain a Scriptural basis for its doctrines. Between 1517, when Luther published his reforming Theses, and 1563, the end of the Roman Catholic Council of Trent (Trento, north Italy), this ferment cracked open the Church's old structure, and enthusiasm for the New Learning of the Renaissance challenged the Church's claim to exclusive wisdom. One of the greatest struggles was over the circulation of scriptures and religious instruction in the vernacular; printed books and pamphlets, the spread of popular education and the rise of a prosperous middle class upset the whole ecclesiastical balance, and also had drastic political results in England and on the continent.

Much of northern Europe followed the lead of Martin Luther, the energetic, pragmatic, authoritarian, passionate, anti-semitic, north German; western Protestantism (including Scottish Presbyterianism, and some English sects) was more influenced by John Calvin. Both held that redemption from man's sins came only from faith in Christ and not, as in Catholic teaching,) from good deeds or prayers for the dead; Calvinists believed that only the elect - those chosen by God at some point early in the world's history - could be saved. Calvin, an intellectual and democratic northern Frenchman in Geneva, was intensely concerned with bringing godliness back to earth, calling in aid of the Church the power of the State to control private behaviour. Neither of these groups was tolerant of dissenting opinion.

Luther's reforming and controversial passion and his love of music and scripture led to the great tradition of chorale writing and harmonised singing in German and Scandinavian Protestant churches; his love of language inspired the develoment of a standard, literary, German. By the next century Lutheran piety had cooled, but the local churches were very strong, and great hymns were written during plague and wartime disaster: Lutheran pastors wrote *Wachet auf* ('Sleepers, wake', or 'Wake O wake'), *Nun danket* ('Now thank we all our God'), and *Lobe den Herrn* ('Praise to the Lord, the Almighty'). Schütz and Bach wrote psalms, motets, cantatas and Passions for Lutheran churches - but by then the Pietist verse used in aria and chorale was in danger of self-indulgence. Singing and literary merit were also important to Calvin; he wrote and commissioned metrical versions of the Psalms (which spread to Elizabethan England), but hymns were not allowed because their texts were not Scriptural. Harmony was excluded until the nineteenth century, though hymn-books today give us charming harmonised settings by Louis Bourgeois (born 1523), the main composer of the Genevan Psalter, which was not then allowed to show harmony. Calvinist singing, in unison and unaccompanied, could be slow and dour; echoes of this remain in some Scottish Presbyterian churches.

Both Protestant groups denied the Pope's final authority over the Church. The German states of the Holy Roman Empire were sharply divided between Catholic and Protestant. In 1555 the Peace of Augsburg provided that the secular ruler should decide the state's religion ('*cuius regio eius religio*'): but the Calvinists, centred in Switzerland, were left out. The Emperor, Charles V, could not achieve the unity which would allow him to follow Charlemagne's aim of setting up a Christian State, supported by the spiritual power of the Pope. Germany and (mainly Catholic) France remained apart. After the disastrous Thirty Years' War and the Peace of Westphalia, 1648, the Emperor, France and Sweden agreed that each prince's religion should determine religion in most of the Continent (and that princes should not change their religion), but that certain areas could be Calvinist. This religion remained strong in reformed Churches in Switzerland, France, the Netherlands, in Scottish Presbyterianism and in some English and Welsh non-conformist Churches.

Roman Catholicism

The 'Counter-Reformation' in the Roman Catholic Church began as a response to Luther's criticism and then schism. From the 1520s new religious Orders grew up: Capuchins and others, then the Society of Jesus, whose Jesuit priests became from 1540 the spearhead both of reform and of attempts to extirpate Protestantism. From 1545 to 1563 the Council of Trent formulated important reforms of organisation and of doctrine which Pope Pius IV promulgated with his 'Profession of the Tridentine Faith'. Initial hopes of a reconciliation with the Protestants had vanished, and the lands of the Emperor Charles V and his son Philip II of Spain faced continued religious and political strife. There were religious wars in France in mid-century; war in the Netherlands from 1568 to 1648, with the involvement of the Spanish Inquisition; and the Thirty Years' War in Germany from 1618 left the area divided between a Catholic Rhineland and the south, and the Protestant north.

The ancient doctrines and practices of the Catholic Church, with these reforms, continued under the bishops of the various national Churches, under Papal leadership and with a degree of tension between Roman wishes for uniformity and the local Uses or variations followed by the French and others. The Council had insisted on greater clarity in the style, and particularly the words, of polyphonic music. But in the seventeenth century baroque music grew up, with solos and instruments. Cathedrals and wealthy churches and princely courts continued to engage musicians, demanding music in their favourite style (as also in Lutheran Germany). In fashionable churches the Mass might degenerate into a public concert, and poor but showy music was widely accepted, especially in Italy. Pope Pius X introduced in 1903 wide reforms of Church life, including the music; ornate music was to go and be replaced by the revived Gregorian chant (*Motu proprio*: see my *Singing in Latin*, 301-310). The Second Vatican Council in 1962-5 allowed vernacular liturgies, and this was taken up so widely that in most places the Latin services and their heritage of music were abandoned.

The Church in the British Isles

In England (and in Wales and Ireland) the King kept control of church doctrine and organisation, following Henry VIII's break with Papal authority. He did not aim at Protestant reform, but some changes were made, and English began to be used in some services, with clear and simple music. A Protestant regime followed (1547-53) under the child-king Edward VI; then for five years the Catholic regime was swiftly restored under Mary I (who married Philip II of Spain, the scourge of Protestantism in the Netherlands). Under Elizabeth there was a cautious but definite move away from Catholicism, and she and the entire realm were excommunicated by the Pope. Many Catholics fled to the Continent, their descendants returning only when toleration grew, 250-300 years later. Others, including Tallis and Byrd, remained as 'recusants', subject to punishment but secretly worshipping (often in the chapels of great houses), sometimes even avoiding the compulsory attendance at their parish churches.

In 1580 the Jesuits sent missionaries to help recusant priests to reclaim England for the Catholic Church. This increased English nervousness about political and military attacks, and action against Catholics became more severe; the defeat of the Spanish Armada in 1588 gave some relief. Many of Byrd's motets reflect his feelings about the oppression of his Church; often they use the loss of Jerusalem by the exiled Jews as a metaphor (whose meaning can hardly have remained secret): *Turn our captivity, Ne irascaris, Tribulationes civitatum, Sacerdotes Domini,* even *Laetentur caeli ... quia Dominus noster veniet, et pauperum suorum miserebitur* ('for the Lord our God shall come again, and have mercy upon his people') ; and Tallis's and Byrd's 'Lamentations'.

In some areas there was popular support for the reformed services from the *Book of Common Prayer*, using the eloquent and understandable English that Cranmer had provided (he was burnt in Mary's reign), and well-loved metrical psalms, introduced largely by Protestants who had fled to the Continent from persecution in England. But Duffy's *The Stripping of the Altars* makes a strong case for the underlying and persistent Catholicism of much of the country; parishes were obedient to the Crown's orders but the loss of the old ways was deeply felt, and in many parishes adornments were hidden in houses in the hope that they might be brought back into use, as they had been in Mary's reign.

What then did the worshippers believe as they sang, for instance, 'Lord, have mercy upon us'? Was it what they earlier meant in *Kyrie eleison*? Let us spell it out in the words of a favourite English anthem (by John Hilton the elder, organist of Trinity College, Cambridge, from 1594):

Lord, for thy tender mercies' sake lay not our sins to our charge: but forgive that is past, and give us grace to amend our sinful lives.

The supplicant is perhaps asking two things. First, that God will not punish him in this world. God's 'providence' was held to intervene in everyday life: a believer stricken by disease or disaster would know that nothing happened without God's permission, and would search himself to find the moral defect which had provoked God's wrath (Thomas, 90, 96, 100). Natural remedies, for the plague for instance, were of little use without repentance and the leading of a godly life. Secondly, the supplicant asks that when he is judged after death, Christ's mercy (effected through his sacrifice for man on the Cross) may relieve him of the weight of his accumulated sins. The doctrine of Purgatory had been abolished at the Reformation: the question therefore was whether the dying man could expect unlimited Hell or immediate Heaven.

The Protestant doctrine was that souls are freed from sin only by faith in Christ, and not by good works. As in Catholic doctrine, this required sincere repentance - changing one's life through the power of God's grace. So - if the words were taken seriously at all - the call for forgiveness and grace for amendment of life was vital. But in 'Lord, for thy tender mercies' sake' the words pass so quickly and suavely that one may suspect that nothing too anguished or decisive was intended: compare the jabbing suspensions in *Dona nobis pacem* at the end of Byrd's 'Mass for Four Voices'. In the English anthem we contribute to a beautiful and pious atmosphere; an over-emphatic interpretation would disrupt the artistry of the piece.

Had the fear of torment after death receded, taking with it the need for a real supplication? It seems likely that many worshippers were somewhat passive in their worship because old forms and teachings had been abolished under Edward VI in favour of new compulsory doctrine, then the old forms restored by Mary, and after her death soon again forbidden. Bending a piece of metal backwards and forwards weakens it through fatigue; perhaps the Church of England came to suffer from doctrinal fatigue: and furthermore Renaissance humanism could have helped to cool religious fervour.

If so, Anglican England may have differed not only from Catholic Europe and its own past, but from the Lutheran and Calvinist countries: and our Judgment about this may affect the way we sing post-Reformation music. How much of it was heart-felt and thoroughly committed? The decline in the energy of the Church of England led to the emergence of Methodism in the eighteenth century under John Wesley, and to many great hymns.

From the start of Elizabeth's reign there was strong Puritan pressure for more radical reform of doctrine and worship; this included objection to organs, and sometimes an antipathy to sensuous beauty, visual or aural. Under Charles I Archbishop Laud was hostile to this movement, seeking to move the Church back towards Catholic practices. The struggles of the Civil War (1642-51) and the Commonwealth period had a strong religious element, with the temporary supremacy of Presbyterianism. Cathedrals were closed, choirs were disbanded and music books destroyed, although Cromwell himself gave some support to singers.

With the Restoration of the monarchy in 1660 the emphasis moved towards soloistic and instrumental music, Charles II having spent his years in exile in the magnificence of Louis XIV's Court at Versailles. But ordinary congregations were not affected by this; they loved metrical psalms, with the whole congregation singing in unison or in simple harmony around the 'tenor' (the baritone part bearing the melody, which the men could roar out). During the eighteenth century choirs with treble boys developed, following the example of the Foundling Hospital boys who had greatly impressed Handel. Fashionable churches adopted choral services and looked down on congregational singing; they did not want the uncultured singing of the common herd. Once trained boys were employed, it was natural for the melody in hymns to move to the treble line. (This neglected area of church music is explored in N. Temperley, *The Music of the English Parish Church*, Cambridge, 1979.) I suspect that over a couple of centuries the loss of the old 'tenor' encouraged many 'common men' to detach themselves from the active life of the church. Singing the treble part an octave down was no substitute unless the man's voice was high, and an Englishman, unless he had learnt singing as a choirboy, could not usually sing a harmony part, even if Welshmen could.

Let me revert to what congregations felt they were singing about. I have explained my guess that churchgoers may have become confused and fatigued in the beliefs expected of them, but at least the doctrine of hellfire and the Devil survived strongly and was not eradicated by the Reformation. The Elizabethan Communion service included a warning by the priest that evil livers should not come to the table 'lest ... the Devil ... bring you to destruction both of body and soul'. Thomas, recording this, goes on 'The battle with Satan and his hierarchy of demons was thus a literal reality for most devout Englishmen'; mighty winds, thunder and lightning were commonly thought to be signs that the Devil was around and at work (561-3). But God was good, and powerful.

In the first half of the seventeenth century William Laud, later Archbishop of Canterbury, led a High Church movement against Calvinism and Puritanism, seeking to restore earlier liturgical practices centred on the altar and the Eucharist: he over-reached himself in trying to enforce a new liturgy in Scotland, and he was impeached by Parliament and later executed.

By the time we come to Restoration music, after the Civil War, one may suspect that some of the seriousness of belief was fading, perhaps especially in the sophisticated London circles for which Blow and Purcell wrote their church music. The Catholicism of the later Stuarts led to the 'Glorious Revolution' of 1688, and in the next reign Queen Mary's funeral aroused popular emotion and involved great ceremony and stately music. In the Church of England there was a High Church revival in Anne's reign, but for many years there was a decline - although in secular matters in each parish the vicar and churchwardens were still a very powerful force.

Under the 1662 Act of Uniformity many ministers who dissented from the demands of the new *Book of Common Prayer* were ejected from their livings, and non-conformist churches of various denominations grew up despite the obligation to attend the parish church. From 1690 freedom of worship was restored to non-conformists, and many great hymns were written by Isaac Watts and others.

Between 1778 and 1829 Roman Catholics were gradually emancipated, though Irish political and religious troubles remained unsolved.

The Methodist movement was started within the Church of England in the late 1730s by John and Charles

Wesley; hymns were a vital part of their mission, which brought a rebirth of religious feeling among great numbers of working-class and lower middle-class people whose lives had been uprooted by industrial and rural developments. A little later the Evangelical Revival started in the Church of England; for us it is notable for the hymns written at Olney by John Newton ('Glorious things of thee are spoken') and the poet William Cowper ('God moves in a mysterious way'). Then from the 1840s there was another great revival of religion and hymnody, this time on the Anglo-Catholic side. This started in Oxford but spread both to prosperous suburb and poor inner-city parishes; the vicar of the University Church, John Henry Newman, converted to Roman Catholicism in 1845 and later became a Cardinal. Elgar set part of Newman's long poem *The Dream of Gerontius* as an oratorio, which in turn (see p. 83f) gave our hymn 'Praise to the Holiest in the height'.

But hymns and psalms need a chapter on their own.

7. PSALMS AND HYMNS

Together psalms and hymns made up a great part of the traditional music of the Church, whether Roman Catholic (especially the monastic services with their weekly cycle of psalms), Anglican or non-conformist. In the last 30-40 years most Anglican churches have concentrated on Parish Communion services at the expense of Matins and Evensong, with their monthly cycle of psalms, said or sung. Anyone who has sung the psalms regularly, as plainchant or as Anglican chant, or even read them regularly, will feel their special quality and will never lose a love for them, and will want new generations to have the chance to use them in worship. Hymns have survived and developed, and few of us are without a large selection of favourite (and unfavourite) hymns.

This chapter touches on some of the problems that singers have in coming to a full appreciation of the words of psalms and hymns. I find myself that concentrating on reading a lower musical part takes one's mind away from the words - perhaps sopranos do not have this problem? - and at worst the words become a nuisance that one puts in because the choirmaster insists. I shall suggest how we can ensure that the sung words are a full part of our worship, and give a few examples which may be useful when readers consider other hymns they intend to sing.

The Psalms

Psalms have been sung from very early times in the Christian Church: but the Jewish Christians of course knew them from their own worship.) They were 'the hymn-book of the Second Temple' (520 BC-AD 70), and many may have been sung in the First Temple (built by Solomon in the tenth century BC, destroyed 586 BC). They are Hebrew poems: the Authorised Version of the Bible and the Prayer Book print them as prose, but the verses are always in two parts separated by a colon. (One 'half' is sometimes very long, because some of the Hebrew verses were divided into three.) So the form is clear, and it is reflected in the way they are sung in Gregorian or in Anglican chant -

I will lift up mine eyes unto the hills:
      [in the plainchant tradition, here follows a pause]
   from whence cometh my help.

The Psalms have been conventionally (but not for the most part historically) ascribed to King David, Solomon's father. They cover the whole range of relations between God (Jehovah) and his people, the Jews. They are pre-Christian, calling for vengeance on the wicked, but like some OT prophetic books they contain passages which have been used in a Christian sense. The Jewish expectation of a Messiah, or Christ, who would be a scion of David's line (Matt. 22, 42) is turned by the writers of the Gospels into a prophecy of the coming and Passion of Christ - 'All they that see me laugh me to scorn ... He trusted in God, that he would deliver him ... ' (Ps. 22, quoted also in Matt. 27, 43). And the opening of this psalm was in the minds of all Jews when Christ's last cry was 'My God, my God, why hast thou forsaken me': they knew the psalms, and thought in those terms.

Monastic services, or Offices, included the whole cycle of 150 psalms each week, mainly at Matins and Vespers. The extent of their use in the Mass, and the refrains or antiphons, varied over time. (On this and much else the reader will find invaluable John Harper's *The Forms and Orders of Western Liturgy*, 69f.; see my App. 4.) Not only monks but cathedral choristers (from boyhood) had to know the Latin Psalter by heart. When Latin services in England were stopped, two psalms, in English, survived to be sung regularly in Matins: the *Venite*, (Ps. 95) and (as alternative to the *Benedictus*, from St Luke) Ps. 100, the *Jubilate*. The new service of Evensong was made up from the monastic Vespers and Compline, and included the whole cycle of psalms each month; *Cantate Domino* and *Deus misereatur* (Ps. 67) were the alternatives respectively to *Magnificat* and *Nunc Dimittis* (both from Luke's Gospel).

The **psalm numbers** I quote are those in the Authorised Version and the *Book of Common Prayer* (and the Hebrew Bible). The corresponding numbers in the Latin Vulgate (and Greek Septuagint) are one less for Pss. 10-147 inclusive, because the Vulgate combines 9 with 10 and 114 with 115, and splits 116 and 147 each into two.

Anglican **chant** derives from harmonised plainchant, common in England in the sixteenth century and used by some Continental composers; later, short harmonised melodies were composed for the purpose. It was only in the nineteenth century that systematic pointing was introduced, varying in different psalters, and the present familiar repertory established.

Hymns

A hymn was originally any sung act of praise to God. 'And when they had sung an hymn' (Mark 14, 26, after the Last Supper) probably refers to the Hallel, certain psalms (113-18) sung by the Jews in the Temple at great festivals like Passover; St Paul writes to the Colossians (3, 16) 'Let the word of Christ dwell in you richly in all wisdom; teaching and admonishing one another in psalms and hymns and spiritual songs, singing with grace in your hearts to the Lord'. Even if we don't subscribe to all that Paul says in Colossians 3, we can safely follow this instruction - though it was a long time before the church in Rome accepted hymns, and similarly (because they were non-biblical) with the Anglican and Calvinist churches.

Early Christian hymns that survive include the *Te Deum* ('We praise thee, O God') and *Gloria in excelsis Deo* ('Glory to God in the highest', the Angelic Hymn, translated from Greek). In the late fourth century St Ambrose expanded the use of hymns, especially to keep up his Milan congregation's spirits at a time of strife with the Arian heresy (see p. 155). His distinctive iambic rhythm (short, long) was widely adopted - as in *O lux beata Trinitas* ('O Trinity of blessed light'). A little later St Benedict included hymns in the services designed for his monastic movement - for instance, at Compline *Te lucis ante terminum*: 'Before the ending of the day'. By the sixth century we have two tunes which are known to go with the hymns (because they were written, in France, for a single event): *Vexilla regis prodeunt* ('The royal banners forward go') and *Pange lingua gloriosi* ('Sing, my tongue, the glorious battle'). One common tradition is to sing these chant-tunes with equal notes, rather than (respectively) short-long and long-short, but we can reasonably be more flexible than that.

In thirteenth-century Italy a long tradition of *Laude spirituali* grew up as a popular form of devotion; this developed into part-singing and even into oratorio. In England hymns or carols were sung between the scenes of the medieval Mystery plays, and in the fifteenth century the simple but highly rhythmic polyphonic carol became popular, both with ordinary people and with the friars who used them for religious teaching - see p. 4 for 'There is no rose'. Carols were sometimes political, like the Agincourt carol, or moral, or folksy; some celebrated Christ's birth: see John Stevens, *Mediæval Carols (Musica Britannica IV)*.

In sixteenth-century Rome Palestrina wrote a polyphonic set of office hymns for the whole of the Church's year, *Hymni totius anni*, which most of us have failed to explore; and he and Lassus wrote sets of offertories. In the north, earlier in the century Isaac provided Propers for the whole year, *Choralis Constantinus*, based on plainchant melodies. (See Appendix 1 for these and other seasonal liturgical music.) Luther wrote *Kirchenlieder* for three to six parts with the plainchant in the tenor, and encouraged enthusiastic congregational singing with the great organ; the chorale form that we know developed out of vernacular hymns written in Germany from the ninth century onwards, from popular song, and from original tunes, some by Luther himself. Johannes Walter's hymn-book of 1524 added five-part harmony, designed to attract youths from lecherous and fleshly songs; and Hans Sachs, poet and *Meistersinger*, was among those who adapted the pre-Reformation words. In Geneva Calvin developed metrical psalms, without harmony or instruments; and he excluded non-biblical texts.

The Church of England also forbade such texts, and to Cranmer's regret did not replace the old hymns which had been sung in the Latin services, except for *Veni creator* - 'Come, Holy Ghost, our souls inspire', which has a tune attributed to Tallis. (Much later, in the Liturgical Revival of the nineteenth century, several Latin hymns came into use in translation.) From 1560 several collections of English metrical psalms appeared, including the *Old Hundredth* ('All people that on earth do dwell'), harmonised from the Genevan Psalter. Around the 1630s an unidentified High churchman complained that the Puritans had replaced the ancient hymns of the Church with 'songs of their own altering and composing, to be sung ... by a company of crude people, cobblers and their wives, and their kitchen-maids and all, that have as much skill in singing, as an ass has to handle a harp' (Temperley, *The Music of the English Parish Church*, 52, a book on which I have drawn heavily).

In 1700 the Crown authorised the use of a Supplement to Tate and Brady's 'New Version' of the Psalter, which contained non-biblical hymns, which then grew in number. Nahum Tate's words of 'While shepherds watched' date from then; we use an older tune, *Winchester Old*, 1591, but there were also more lively ones (*NOBC* has seven tunes). This exuberance displeased the gentry, as did the roaring of the metrical chants, but most of the congregation loved the hymns because they were simple and singable. The tune was in the (low) tenor, and untrained men and women could easily sing it; indeed, they sang so enthusiastically that one reported purpose for the wider use of organs was to keep decorum among the 'discordant multitudes'. There was also a move towards choral training among young working-class men who formed religious societies in the late seventeenth century centred on the SPCK; they sometimes combined with choirs of children from charity schools. Later, 'fuging' tunes became popular, where one voice imitated another after a few notes.

The leadership of the singing had long been the job of the parish clerk, who 'lined out' the psalm by singing each line for the congregation to repeat. Playford in 1690 directed clerks to choose the proper pitch for each tune, 'that thereby you may give the *tune* of your first *note* so as the rest may be sung in the compass of the voice, without *squeaking* above, or *grumbling* below'. In the wealthier parish churches the gentry, who had begun to stay away, began to encourage another kind of singing once they heard what the 'charity children' from the Foundling Hospital in London could do, under skilled musical direction. Choirs of men and boys were modelled on those of cathedrals and collegiate churches. The tune was moved to the treble for the boys (where it still remains, making it difficult for the untrained man's voice). This fashion led to conflict with those who wanted to hold to the old congregational style; and because clergy and gentry had dissociated themselves from the music of the people there had been no synthesis, such as Luther achieved in Germany, between popular music and learned forms. (The same conflict in choosing between congregation-based and choir-led services is painfully felt in some churches today.)

From 1740 some country churches started bands to lead the singing from the west gallery, and a repertory of hymns and devotional songs grew up (now being revived by enthusiastic groups of singers and players here and in America, using 'shape-notes' to help in reading the music: see p. 172). And by the end of the eighteenth century most country churches apart from the extreme north had choirs. One complication was that men and women were segregated in the congregation; a mixed choir needed to be fairly close together, and the west gallery allowed this.

At the same time the High Anglican John Wesley was starting his national mission among non-churchgoing people, and his brother Charles was writing hundreds of hymns which had an immense impact when combined with the redemptive preaching. The men were expected to sing the bass, not duplicate the women's treble. Non-conformist churches were already using hymns newly written by Isaac Watts and others; and in Wales a great tradition of hymn writing and singing grew up. For all these groups the hymn was - and is still - a closely-knit part of the minister's teaching, and to some extent this applies also to the hymns of the Liturgical Revival (the 'Oxford Movement'). But the more familiar we are with hymns, the less we may think about what they meant to say, so that only the first line or so stays with us. Selection of hymns may depend heavily on what people like, and are comfortable with: but familiarity can become complacency. Is this the sort of service which the minister and the church really wants? Christian doctrine is neither complacent nor pain-free, and the hymns, though they may teach, should be a genuine expression of the worshipper's meaning.

We now look at a few hymns to try to uncover the layers of meaning that may be built in, to help the singer and worshipper to discover them in other hymns. I recommend to serious church musicians and clergy three books by the late Erik Routley - *Hymns and Human Life* (HHL): history of hymns and the background of the writers; *Hymns and the Faith* (HF): comments on texts of 49 well-known hymns; *Hymns Today and Tomorrow* (HTT): the language of hymns; how the church should use them.

Let us take four hymns which have started from psalms. First, a metrical psalm which is a very close paraphrase and where we have both sets of words and the tune from 1540/60, **'All people that on earth do dwell'**, from Ps. 100, *Jubilate Deo*. The first verse matches 'O be joyful in the Lord, all ye lands'; the second, 'The Lord, ye know, is God indeed' goes with 'Be ye sure that the Lord he is God'; the third, 'O enter then his gates with praise' with 'O go your way into his gates with thanksgiving'; and 'For why, the Lord our God is good' with 'For the Lord is gracious'. Both versions are lovely writing, and the metrical psalm has become one of the most enduring of hymns - though its meaning suffered when *Hymns A&M* altered 'Him serve with mirth' to 'with fear' - God as a Victorian patriarch?. We often find shifts of meaning in old hymns; 'mirth' did not imply a jest. (See also HF, 19.)

Contemporaneous tunes are not common, but another goes with **'Praise the Lord! ye heavens, adore him'**, the adaptation of Ps. 148, written for the Foundling Hospital and other children's choirs of the Evangelical revival to sing with Haydn's tune *Austria* (HF, 1-6). This great hymn of praise is close to the psalm, but with a significant change: at the end of the psalm - which is of course pre-Christian - God exalts the horn of the children of Israel that serve him (the Jewish nation, not all mankind, is made fertile): but the hymn promises salvation ('Sin and death shall not prevail'). This can be defended as a new understanding of the contact between God and man, and of the power of God's love - but is not the shift to Christianity more radical than that? The hymn transmutes the tribal victory of the psalm into a Christian victory, available (I think) to all, not just the 'elect'of strict Calvinism.

'O worship the King' was paraphrased in 1833 from Ps. 104 (HF, 7-12). But it dodges the unChristian sentiments of the last verse, common in the Psalms. In the *BCP*: 'As for sinners, they shall be consumed out of the earth, and the ungodly shall come to an end: praise thou the Lord, O my soul, praise the Lord'. And the hymn extols the almighty power of God ('His chariots of wrath/ The deep thunder clouds form'); how does this consort with his love and with our free will? (Routley suggests that we may think of 'O measureless might, ineffable love'.) In any case do these potent adjectives not slip past as we sing, with no time for the close attention the argument needs?

The parent psalm, 104, is so powerful and beautiful in the Prayer Book version that adapting it is a surprising liberty. Why don't we sing it, except in choral evensong on the 20th evening? The theological message differs; the Psalmist doesn't try to explain God's ways as the hymn does, but realises he is subject to God's will, whatever that be: he will still praise the Lord while he has his being. (E. Charpentier, *How to read the New Testament*, 99, gives us the intriguing side-light that Ps. 104 is inspired by an Egyptian hymn to the sun god.) But the more likely reason for preferring the version in the hymn is a literary one. The psalm assumes that, like the ancient Hebrews, we are at home with, and receptive to, poetic expression; the hymn has a more familiar form - a versified prose sermon. Using all-too-familiar metaphor it has become part of our background; it steers the congregation somewhere in the right direction. But one should cherish the opportunity to read or chant Ps. 104, and to absorb and enjoy its words.

There may be several hymns based on the same psalm: there is a rich mixture for **Ps. 23** (*Dominus regit me*). The *Book of Common Prayer* (BCP) and the Authorised Version (AV) differ; we chant the former (which has the significant phrase 'He shall convert my soul': AV 'He restoreth'). We have at least four paraphrases, and which we like is a litmus test of one's temperament. This is complicated by the qualities of the tunes habitually used.

Crimond (**'The Lord's my shepherd, I'll not want'**) was used at Her Majesty's wedding in 1947. It was popularised by the Glasgow Orpheus Choir, and its sentimentality has earned it a wide following.

'The King of love my shepherd is' (HF 63-8) is a competent and moving Victorian version which introduces NT and ecclesiastical language - the Good Shepherd, the Cross to guide me, the chalice flowing; and Christ's house as an eternal home.

'The God of love my shepherd is' is George Herbert's paraphrase (not written as a hymn but well suited by the eighteenth-century tune *University*). It is a jewel, using simple language as a real poet can; and the last verse, 'Surely thy sweet and wondrous love', is for me the last word.

'The Lord my pasture shall prepare' is Addison's version. With the tune *Surrey*, composed soon afterwards, it has plenty of period charm: but changes in habit of speech have overtaken it. Even Anglicans don't faint in the sultry glebe except on a hot Sunday School sports day, if such still exist; and one needs iron self-control not to smile at 'Thy friendly crook shall give me aid, And guide me through the dreadful shade' - and by that time the meaning has gone. It is a long way from the vivid BCP/AV verse 'Yea, though I walk through the valley of the shadow of death, I will fear no evil'.

(HF 65 also refers to three versions by Isaac Watts, which also make a transition from the Psalm to Christian thought.)

What may lie behind the words

Just as hymn-writers use familiar psalms as building-blocks, Gospel writers, especially Matthew, use OT prophecies as the *authority* for what they think must have happened (Matthew 1, 22, on Mary, Joseph and the Holy Ghost: 'Now all this was done, that it might be fulfilled which was spoken of the Lord by the prophet') or the *explanation* of what they say did happen (2, 15: the Holy Family stayed in Egypt 'that it might be fulfilled which was spoken of the Lord by the prophet, saying, Out of Egypt have I called my son'). Either of these uses of prophecy helps the Evangelist to authenticate Jesus as the true, not a false, Messiah. The hymn-writers were imbued with the whole of Biblical history and thought, which they combined with their own religious experience to enhance the worship of their congregations. We are mostly not so familiar or erudite as they were, and we may miss some of their Biblical or theological references.

A simple case is 'O God of Bethel, by whose hand/ Thy people still are fed'. Why Bethel, and how does food come in? Jacob wanted a wife; his father Isaac sent him from Beersheba to Haran, 500 miles north-east, to find one of his cousins. On the way he lay down for the night, using stones for his pillows, and dreamed of a ladder to heaven; the Lord promised him that land, from which his seed should spread and bless all the families of the earth. Jacob woke and called the place Beth-el ('house of God'), and vowed that if God would be with him, keep him in the way he ought to go, and feed and clothe him, 'then shall the Lord be my God'. Routley explores (HF, 43-50) how Doddridge, the non-conformist, transmutes this ancient covenant into a Christian image. (Q: I ought to remember all this, but where do I look? A: Genesis 28. Q: How do I know it's there? A: Start with 'Bethel' in a Concordance.)

The author's references can be more obscure. The **Rock of Ages**, which the Revd. Augustus Toplady knew as a minute cleft in a Mendip combe, does not feature in the Authorised Version. But Routley (in HF) suggests that Isaiah 26, 4 ('in the Lord Jehovah is everlasting strength') may also be translated from the Hebrew as 'is the Rock of ages'; then the Rock of ages is turned into Christ in whom we can shelter; and a stream gushes forth (as for the Israelites in the desert in Exodus 17), which becomes 'Christ crucified for the release upon the world of God's forgiveness'. But behind the young Toplady's dazzling manipulation of ideas into a hymn which gives comfort and strength lurked a virulent argument with John Wesley about God, evil and free will, schism and religious dictatorship; an entertaining account is in HHL 105-9.

So we cannot always rely on the words and their Biblical references alone; we may need to know something about the writer - which would have been common knowledge at the time. Again, what type of belief should we read into **'City of God, how broad and far'**?

1. City of God, how broad and far
Outspread thy walls sublime!
The true thy chartered freemen are
Of every age and clime.

2. One holy Church, one army strong,
One steadfast high intent,
One voice to raise one triumph-song,
One king omnipotent.

3. How purely hath thy speech come down
From man's primeval youth!
How grandly hath thine empire grown
Of freedom, love, and truth!

4. How gleam thy watch-fires through the night
With never-fainting ray!
How rise thy towers, serene and bright,
To meet the dawning day!

5. In vain the surges' angry shock,
In vain the shifting sands;
Unharmed upon the eternal rock
The eternal city stands.

One can note that v. 2 emphasises the *one* militant and triumphant (Roman) church, and v. 3 the continuity of

(Apostolic) doctrinal tradition (though 'primeval youth' uses perhaps poetic licence). V. 5 gives us the surges of schism from the true Church, the rock on which it is built and on which the Pope's claim to authority rests (*Tu es Petrus*; Matt. 16, 18f). The last line of the hymn would then point to Rome, the Eternal City. So is this, as might appear, a hymn of well-worn Catholic doctrine? No; Routley shows that it was a manifestation of militant liberalism. The writer, Samuel Johnson (d. 1882: not our Dr Johnson) was an American Unitarian writing to emphasise that the Church comprised all men of goodwill, and that no creed or covenant was required, discarding the Roman doctrine of the Church (HHL, 115f, HF, 254-6); the imagery is literary and optimistic, not biblical. The 'eternal city' then is not Rome but Zion, the citadel in Jerusalem, metaphorically God's holy hill. (In v. 1 the City of God is then Jerusalem, the holy city, the redeemed Church.)

So, as for 'Rock of ages', we should not rely on the hymn's words alone: metaphor enriches abstract thought by encouraging free association of ideas, but at the expense of possible misinterpretation of a writer's meaning. (Routley's chapters on mythology and allegory, HTT 48-89, help to get us into gear.)

A great hymn, undoubtedly Catholic, which assumes knowledge of an author's other writings is **'Praise to the Holiest in the height'**. John Henry Newman had been Vicar of the University Church at Oxford, became a leader of the High Church Liturgical Revival, moved to the Roman Church in 1845 and eventually became a Cardinal. Routley discusses its 'vast and imaginative content' in HF, 281-92. The hymn's immediate source is Elgar's *The Dream of Gerontius*, but behind that lies Newman's long poem of that name. In the fifth of seven cantos Gerontius ('little old man' in Greek) is dying; his agony as he receives communion is recounted by the Angel - the flame of everlasting love burns before it transforms. Then one 'choir of angelicals' sings part of the hymn, which has 35 verses. With dialogue in between, four other choirs of angelicals continue the hymn with the whole story of Adam's Fall and the war between good and evil, God and Satan. Each section starts with the first verse, but the poem ends not with that verse, as in the hymn-books, but with the coming of the second Adam. This is Christ, who rescues flesh and blood, and endures the double agony, 'To teach his brethren, and inspire/ To suffer and to die'. Routley ends by quoting C.S. Lewis's words after witnessing the death of a friend: 'It was the idea of death that was changed'. The feeling in this hymn is intense. No words are wasted; each line needs to be pondered, before and after singing.

A very different Newman hymn is **'Firmly I believe'**. The words need close attention for a different reason:

1. Firmly I believe and truly/ God is Three and God is One;
And I next acknowledge duly/ Manhood taken by the Son.
        [vv. 2-4 follow]
5. And I hold in veneration/ For the love of him alone,
Holy Church as his creation,/ And her teachings as his own.
        [v. 6 follows]

This has no literary claims. It is a simple Trinitarian creed in mnemonic form with a didactic pupose; those singing it are to absorb, and accept, the doctrine it teaches. (In rather the same way children used to be taught to chant, in order, the names of the books of the OT, and the multiplication tables.) The vital point comes in v. 5 - we are to accept whatever the Church teaches as if it is Christ's own doctrine, because he created and gave authority to the Church (see p. 83 on *Tu es Petrus*). Now for those of us whose compulsion to honesty (and spiritual pride?) requires that a solemn declaration demands understanding and personal acceptance, delegating decisions on divine truth to the human and earthly Church is akin to blasphemy. (The Church used to claim a wider monopoly of truth: this is how Galileo got into such trouble.) To a Catholic, Anglo- or Roman, acceptance of doctrine is a natural consequence of loyalty to the Church into which one has been baptised, and v. 5 is a joyful affirmation. But others may choose not to sing this verse.

Here are three deeply-felt hymns whose words have very serious meanings for the singer. Charles Wesley's **'Jesu, lover of my soul,**/ Let me to thy bosom fly' (HF, 175-180) is a challenge, not a hymn of easy comfort. I ask that Jesu will support and comfort me: but there is an enemy within - 'False and full of sin I am'. We realise that a radical change (a conversion) is the only way out of our fear, and that only Jesu's 'plenteous grace' can help us to achieve this. (The powerful metaphor of water keeps recurring: the nearer waters are rolling, endangering and frightening us; grace comes in 'healing streams', and we ask that Jesu, as the fountain of life, shall spring up within our heart when we freely take of him.) Given a real involvement with the words, the magnificent tune 'Aberystwyth', if we have the sense to choose it, will vibrate right through us: it will not be just a wonderful sing-through.

'Just as I am' (HF, 181-4) is also a hymn of conversion, because we realise that 'as I am' will not do for ever; but Christ is ready to receive us when we come to him. When we accept his invitation, however poor, wretched, blind we are, we convert from 'as I am', and prove (make trial of) the breadth, length and depth of that free love.

Lastly (HF, 111-17), Isaac Watts's great hymn **'When I survey the wondrous Cross'**. (This originally continued 'Where the young prince of glory died' - how much more telling than 'On which the prince'.) We sacrifice 'All the vain things that charm us most'; we are 'dead to all the globe' as 'His dying crimson like a robe/ Spreads o'er his body on the tree'; and 'Love so amazing, so divine,/ Demands my soul, my life, my all'. Do we mean anything when we sing this? If not, should we presume to sing these great words?

Do these hymns say what we mean?

In these last three hymns, singing their *meaning* would involve a decision for *conversion*. I use that unfashionable word to suggest that unless we merely skid over the words as a familiar abracadabra, we are letting ourselves in for a change of life, which may be dramatic, as when someone goes up to give his name in at Billy Graham's rostrum, or heroically brave, as when a Christian is challenged by a hostile power and thrown to the lions or (as nowadays) tortured or killed. Or the change can be organic and gentle, but decisive and whole: try reading slowly through the seventeenth-century words of **'My song is love unknown'**. The first verse realises the power of Christ's love (it changes the unlovely); why should he do this for *me*? Then we hear that he was ignored, then feted, then vengefully killed: why so, given his deeds of healing? He suffers to save his foes from suffering; his tomb was given by a stranger, 'but mine the tomb wherein he lay': Christ has entered into me. 'Here might I stay and sing' comes finally as a gentle decision of love and dedication, coming out of the poem's reasoning, and from the heart:

This is my Friend,
    In whose sweet praise
    I all my days
Could gladly spend.

How do we choose hymns?

When a service is being planned, are hymns rotated more or less automatically according to season, or are they seen as a part of the preparation of the teaching which the minister intends for that day? One can imagine a minister thinking 'It's a long time since we sang "When I survey", and it's Good Friday, and people will feel deprived if we don't sing it, but are we really ready for that?' He might go on to think 'No, I'm not going to encourage people to sing what they don't mean. And anyway, if they do, it's habit-building, and they'll go on taking no notice of the words.' Or he may think 'The more they say or sing these words, the more it will permeate their minds and being. They will come, I trust, gradually to know the truth through this repetition.'

This second attitude, the instructional, is perhaps more common on the catholic side of the Church; the first, with its dependence on the progress of the worshipper's own response to the theme of the service, may reflect an evangelical or a non-conformist approach.

Clearly this is a matter of policy that each minister has to decide on: and in many churches the congregation could usefully think deeply about it, and advise. (See Routley's trenchant chapter on the choice of hymns, HTT, 106-28.)

Change and decay

Hymn-books have been under revision for well over a century. They have been subject to waves of fashion; some less-worthy hymns disappear, but congregations become used to them - is there not now a tendency to nostalgia for the 'pop' of their 1960s' youth? New hymns are always needed; in this century these have required less Biblical familiarity than the hymns of the seventeenth to nineteenth centuries, but can be prosaic and worthy when they confront the social and political problems of the secular world.

A distinguished contribution to the move into the twentieth century was made in 1899 by the *Yattendon Hymnal*, under the leadership of Robert Bridges, later to be Poet Laureate. A care for simple and noble words and tunes challenged 'the debased hymnody of that era' (Preface to *Songs of Praise*, 1931 edn.), and this led in 1906 to the *English Hymnal*. An example of those hymns is **'Rejoice, O land, in God thy might'**, to the good broad eighteenth-century tune *Wareham*.

Soon afterwards G.K. Chesterton wrote **'O God of earth and altar'**; the young writer, not yet a Roman Catholic (see HTT, 91-5), lets fly against the imperfections of the nation's citizens at the peak of imperialist confidence. He does not need biblical allusions: he can speak like an OT prophet, and no words are wasted:

1. O God of earth and altar,/ Bow down and hear our cry;
Our earthly rulers falter,/ Our people drift and die;
The walls of gold entomb us,/ The swords of scorn divide:
Take not thy thunder from us,/ But take away our pride.

2. From all that terror teaches,/ From lies of tongue and pen,
From all the easy speeches/ That comfort cruel men,
From sale and profanation/ Of honour and the sword,
From sleep and from damnation,/ Deliver us, good Lord!

3. Tie in a living tether/ The prince and priest and thrall,
Bind all our lives together,/ Smite us and save us all;
In ire and exultation,/ Aflame with faith, and free,
Lift up a living nation,/ A single sword to thee.

Simce the second World War we have had a flood of
hymns and 'choruses' designed to appeal to modern youth.
One which comes off better than most is Sidney Carter's
'Lord of the Dance', which is not prosaic nor bathetic; like
the ballad carol 'Tomorrow shall be my dancing day' (see
p. 98) it combines the ancient religious use of dance (long
frowned on by the Church) with references to the
legendary understanding of the life and death of Christ.
(We may bear in mind the use of movement and drama in
the medieval music-dramas, combined in the mystery plays
with humour and lay participation: see p. 32.)

Unfortunately many other musical offerings are of
inferior quality, and butcher any worth-while words they
are applied to: the Taizé chants, on the other hand, both
preserve good taste and attract young and older people
through their quiet and devout repetitiveness; and there
are good modern hymns in *Rejoice and Sing* (Oxford, for the
URC).

We often sing well-loved hymns which are not really
the best we can offer in the worship of God. The trouble
often arises from the tyranny of the convention of rhyming.

In **'Once in royal David's city'** Mrs Alexander starts with a shed for the baby's bed, and makes Mary a 'Mother mild' in order to rhyme with 'child'; she finishes by rhyming us into a quite boring account of heaven: 'Where like stars his children crowned/ All in white shall wait around'. **'Jerusalem the golden'** is a translation of Bernard of Cluny's *Urbs Sion aurea* by J.M. Neale, a distinguished High Church hymn-writer. But keeping a set metre and providing a succession of English rhymes (though for alternate lines only) lead him into trouble where he has nothing significant to say:

They stand, those halls of Sion/ *Conjubilant* with song ...
The daylight is serene/ The pastures of the blessèd/ Are decked in glorious *sheen*.

The falling last line of the familiar tune (*Ewing*) adds to the insignificance of 'glorious sheen', and later of 'in robes of white'. Is this form of imagery of a future heavenly life so valuable that we must go on singing the hymn? And if we can conceive a ratio of meaning to verbiage, how does 'Jerusalem the golden' compare with Chesterton's 'O God of earth and altar'?

Let us stand up against the assumption that ugliness and emptiness don't matter so long as the words are to be *sung*: and against what must lie behind this attitude - that we don't really *mean* what we sing.

Incidentally, who, I wonder, changed the meaning in that great Welsh hymn 'Guide me, O thou great Jehovah' by substituting 'great Redeemer' in Anglican hymn-books?

Another view

On very kindly reading the draft of this chapter my friend Richard Jeffery produced this note, which I commend to my readers' attention as a contribution to informed controversy - in which I hope they will join:

I can't resist saying that I don't agree in these cases. 'Jerusalem the golden' is a clumsy hymn, probably the original [part of Hora novissima, by Bernard of Cluny, 12th. c.] as much as the translation, but 'conjubilant with song' is a fine line suggesting separate individuals jubilating with and to each other (which is quite lost in the emendation 'all jubilant'), and there's something of the same in 'The song of them that triumph, the shout of them that feast' - it comes in very few of the words of the standard hymns (another is in the original version of 'Hills of the North', 'Shout, while ye journey home! Songs be in every mouth'), much more in the words of the Psalms: 'Make a cheerful noise to the God of Jacob'. To repudiate this would be to move towards rejecting untrained singing in church altogether: these words are saying it's our right and duty all to rejoice - as musically as we can, but not worrying about our perfect adequacy.

I've always loved 'O God of earth and altar', but on consideration I think this is primarily because of the magnificent tune [King's Lynn] and V.W.'s fine harmonization (especially the astonishing single touch of modulation and added rhythm three-quarters of the way through); the words of verse 2 are very fine, particularly the great lines 3-4 ['From all the easy speeches/ That comfort cruel men'], but I think verses 1 and 3 are seriously over the top and out of control, as Chesterton occasionally was; they're impressive as personal expression, but as considered words for a congregation to sing they have something questionable in almost every line. If we address God, oddly, as 'of earth and altar', why

91

suggest that he needs to bow down to hear us? Is 'falter' appropriate for our rulers? (I thought G.K.C. usually regarded them as persisting obstinately in unjust courses.) In what sense do our people 'drift'? Who are 'we', if we're neither 'our rulers' nor 'our people'? Why are 'swords' used three times, first in the vague and clumsy 'swords of scorn', in verses 2-3 to image the doubtfully Christian concepts of personal honour and warrior zeal? If we're to be made a living nation and a single sword to God, why is 'ire' wanted - are we all to rush off to drive the heathen out of Jerusalem? I don't think it stands questioning nearly as well as Blake's 'And did those feet'.

8. CHRISTMAS MUSIC

We sing for Advent, Christmas and Epiphany several kinds of music: medieval carols (see p. 73), with burden before, between and after the verses, known from manuscript sources; ancient Latin, German or French hymns, often in translation; ballad carols, often of ancient origin and transmitted as folk-song, mostly retrieved in modern times; motets, anthems, cantatas and oratorios; and those hymns of the last three centuries which are often loosely known as 'carols'.

Many of us have on our shelves the 1928 *Oxford Book of Carols* ('*OBC*'), perhaps accumulating dust under copies of the handy *Carols for Choirs* (1961 onwards). It is refreshing to read Dr Percy Dearmer's erudite and enthusiastic Preface (v-xix) for its account of the emergence of what he broadly groups as carols, supplemented by the near-illegible but fascinating footnotes through the book; given his insights we may decide to try out some of the neglected carols. Then there is a comprehensive survey by Erik Routley in *The English Carol*. For *The New Oxford Book of Carols* (*NOBC*, 1992), and its shorter version (1993), the editors have unearthed exciting earlier versions of hymns and carols to go alongside those we are familiar with, and give us scholarly background notes.

How are we to understand the Christmas story?

In this chapter I will explore some of the texts, and try to suggest what our mental stance can be when we are wanting to respond fully to the joy of the words and the music but we are uncomfortable about them as literal history.

93

In the section of Chapter 5 headed 'Mystery, myth and metaphor' (p. 53) I said that most of us were not greatly bothered about whether Portia and Shylock existed as described by Shakespeare. It is more difficult when we come to Gabriel and Mary the future mother of Jesus, the shepherds, the ox and the ass, the wise men from the East, and the rest of what we treasure from early childhood in the Christmas story.

A liberal position would be to say that the Gospel accounts, and the texts drawn from them for carols and hymns, are poetic fictions whose validity for us lies in the message of hope for mankind's redemption and not in the declaration of belief in exact historical fact. On the opposite wing are those who maintain that the source of what we know, and (if we are Christians) are to believe, is precisely that which is written in the Gospels and certain other books of the NT. This view is difficult to maintain when the writers of the Gospels differ: Matthew follows the birth at Bethlehem by the visit of the wise men, the Holy family's flight into Egypt, their return after Herod's death to Israel and then to Nazareth, whereas Luke follows the birth with the adoration by the shepherds, the visit to the Temple in Jerusalem and the return to Nazareth. Surely Luke could not have overlooked the time in Egypt and the long journey there and back? Readers can occupy long winter evenings in working out other differences.

I suggest that we have to see the Gospels as a mixture of historical fact (which can at some points be checked with non-biblical historical sources) and parable or legend or poetic drama. The first-century Church was scattered in cities through the Near East, sometimes under active persecution; Christ's followers had been rescued from despair a generation before by the events of the

Resurrection - whatever exact form that took - and they expected an early end of the world, the return of Christ and the coming of the Kingdom of God. The Gospels of Mark, Matthew and Luke saw these as apocalyptic events, and the fact that the world didn't actually come to an end was confusing to them. In John's Gospel, on the other hand, Christ teaches that eternal life is in Him, and that those who believe in Him have it now; the focus is on Easter Day, not a Kingdom of the future. Each Evangelist wanted to convey his own understanding of the wonderful years of Jesus's life on earth, and to guide his readers and hearers towards a Christian life.

More and more Gentiles were coming into the Church, which led to painful controversy (see Acts 15), and Christian teachers needed to meet the disciplines of Greek thought, which was the educated culture of the eastern Mediterranean. But the Evangelists and many of their flock were Jews, and their lives were filled with the many centuries of Jewish history, prophecy and belief recorded in the OT. Historical fact and imaginative story were interwoven and (though we find this difficult to imagine) not clearly distinguished. Matthew and Luke were each individual preachers with their own emphases and theologies, and, as I have mentioned, their accounts differed. The earliest evangelist, Mark, and especially the latest, John, were different again. So we read each in the light of his own general approach: and in singing a carol about shepherds or Orient Kings we need to see why the Evangelist included the story rather than whether history will bear him out.

For some people this will not do: was there a Virgin birth or not? Some thinkers disputed whether Christ's life started when Mary bore him, or from the beginning of time. These logical concerns were more influenced by Greek thought than by the Hebrew approach through prophecy and law; they led to theological strife and to centuries of religious wars. The search for a theological system was never a matter for ordinary believers to decide, though adherents of differing views rioted, as still happens, and the stability of Constantine's empire was imperilled. Once the emperor had got agreement at Nicaea in AD 325, believers were required to endorse in the creeds what the theologians and ecclesiastical politicians had agreed.

The friars' teaching

The rich vein of English carols from the late Middle Ages began when the Church, concerned at the popular love of ballad and dance with secular and often licentious words or pagan overtones, decided to harness it to religious instruction rather than try to stamp it out. The vivid stories about Mary, Joseph, Gabriel, the shepherds, wise men, Herod and the rest, came from the Gospels embroidered with later stories and dogmas. It was particularly the wandering friars of the fourteenth and fifteenth centuries who with energy and devotion caught the imagination of believers as they were instructed in the Catholic faith. We will look at a couple of these to illustrate the thoughts that, through repetition to rhythmic tunes, became familiar even to uneducated people.

OBC 180 tells us about man's fall and redemption:

Adam lay ybounden,
Bounden in a bond;
Four thousand winter
Thought he not too long.
And all was for an apple,
An apple that he took,

As clerkes finden
Written in their book.
Ne had the apple taken been
The apple taken been
Ne had never our Lady
A-been heavene queen.
Blessed be the time
That apple taken was.
Therefore we moun singen
    Deo gracias!

We must recall that people generally had no bibles: only the 'clerkes', the clergy, had them, and only in Latin. Now we are able to look up Genesis 2 and 3 and see that Adam, the first man, was driven out of the Garden of Eden, and prevented for ever from eating of the tree of life because he and Eve had disobeyed God's order not to eat the fruit - the apple - of the tree of knowledge of good and evil (which was not for mere humans). Adam's 'four thousand winters' refers to the time (calculated in the seventeenth century by Archbishop Ussher of Armagh at 4004 years) from the creation to the birth of Christ, who would redeem man. However, the NT takes over from the OT, and our Lady bore the Redeemer of Adam's race, and became Queen of Heaven; the carol points out that she wouldn't have been if the apple had not been taken.

The second carol, *Nova! Nova!* (*Shorter NOBC*, 11), tells the story of the Annunciation. The last verse and the burden is what concerns us now:

Then said the maiden verily:
I am your servant right truly.
Ecce ancilla Domini.
    Nova, nova,
    AVE fit ex EVA.

The 'macaronic' inclusion of Latin phrases with the vernacular does not imply that the hearers or most of the singers understood Latin; probably they picked up a few phrases which they might also hear in the liturgy. And the last line is a small joke: we can make Gabriel's 'Hail Mary', *AVE*, out of the human Eve, *EVA*). This sounds complicated, but it isn't if your mind is brought up to think that way; a fifteenth-century countryman had no rival mental discipline: word-play was not only the preserve of the learned, and we have of course to be ready to interpret the language of religious song in a non-literal fashion.

Christmas carols, as we see from these examples, draw on events commemorated throughout the Christian year. It is natural that there should be lively songs and hymns for other seasons. 'Tomorrow shall be my dancing day' (*OBC* 71) is a ballad, recorded in 1833 but evidently dating from long before that. It is an allegory of Christ's love for the faithful in his Church, his Bride, and his invitation to the heavenly dance. 'Tomorrow' must be Easter, the day of his resurrection, so Christ must be speaking from the tomb on Holy Saturday - far from our usual idea of a Christmas carol. In the verses he tells the story of his life, with careful theological orthodoxy. In v. 1, speaking from before his birth, he wishes that his true love, his Church on earth, will recognise the message of his life, and convert to life in him - the bridegroom calls the bride to the dance. In verse 2 he takes on human nature through the Virgin Birth; verse 3 shows us the *magnum mysterium* - that his life started with the low and unclean (the ox and ass). Verse 4 recounts his baptism, with the voice of the Father and the appearance of the Holy Spirit as a dove (the version in Luke 3, 21f); verse 5 has the ensuing Temptation by the devil, who offered stones for Jesus to show his divine power by turning them into bread (Luke 4, 3); verse 6 has the continued tension with the Jewish religious authorities, verse 7 is a mercenary interpretation of Judas (perhaps inspired by John 12, 6); verses 8 and 9 give the trial and crucifixion, and point to the water and blood as the invitation to the dance. Verse 10 refers to the harrowing of Hell (the medieval doctrine of the reclamation of souls who were already in Purgatory, rather than Hell, possibly expanded from 1 Peter 3, 19). Verse 11 has Christ's Ascension into heaven, where he is consubstantial with the Father, and enables man to complete his redemption. And note that there are eleven verses, standing for the twelve Apostles minus Judas ('Eleven is the eleven who went to heaven'): number symbolism abounds from Biblical writings through the Middle Ages, and was deep in popular lore.

We must face the fact that for many centuries the Church's teaching instilled enmity towards the Jews, arising from the Evangelists' efforts to emphasis the blameworthiness of the Jewish authorities and people, rather than that of the Roman occupying forces, for the death of Jesus. St John's Gospel, 8, 44, has Christ telling his fellow-Jews that their father is the devil, that their will is to do the desire of their father, who was a murderer from the beginning. This and Matthew 27, 25, 'His blood be upon us, and on our children' are not to be taken as historical records but as signs of hostility to those Jews who were not, like the Evangelists, following Jesus. The terrible and unintended result has been the persecution of the Jews, culminating in the Nazi 'Holocaust'. The effect on folk and religious belief is clear in passages like verse 6:

The Jews on me they made great suit,
    And with me made great variance,
Because they loved darkness rather than light,
    To call my true love to the dance.

We have to distance ourselves from this attitude, even though its seeds were sown in St John's Gospel itself. Either we must make it clear that this is merely how an earlier age thought (but we too are guilty sometimes of loving darkness rather than light - cf. John 3, 19), or we have to omit or bowdlerise: the *NOBC* removes 'calculatedly offensive references', and although I dislike sanitisation generally, I think this is right. The same difficulty arises over Passion music: see Chapter 9.

Christmas since the Puritans

The extrovert vigour, earthiness and extravagant imagery of the medieval carol all displeased the Protestant reformers, as did all ceremonies and images. By 1645 the Long Parliament had abolished the observance of Christmas, together with Easter, Whitsun and saints' days, which lay deep in the social as well as religious fabric. Attempts at Puritan hymn-carols need not detain us; after the Restoration the first to live on was 'While shepherds watched', one of a few New Testament hymns attached in 1696 to Tate and Brady's *New Version* of the Psalms; in succeeding centuries this was sung to a variety of tunes: *NOBC* gives seven, including one uncommonly like 'On Ilkley Moor'. The great tune we usually sing, 'Winchester Old', dates from 1592 but only came in with the 1861 edition of *Hymns Ancient and Modern*.

There are two main points about the words of 'While shepherds watched'. In Jewish society shepherds were in low regard, partly because their job was unclean by its nature, and one significance of lambs was that they were sacrificed in the Temple and their blood spilt. The story only comes in Luke (2, 8-20), and only he tells us about the manger and no room at the inn. We can perhaps best see both episodes as Luke's illustration of the *magnum mysterium* of God's incarnation among the lowliest of creation. The other point is that Luke and Matthew put the birth at Bethlehem, instead of Nazareth, because it was clear to them (many years later) that there had been the fulfilment of Micah's prophecy (5, 2) of 'a ruler in Israel' who would come forth from Bethlehem. Luke (and no other evangelist or historian) says that there was a census for which Joseph and Mary had to travel 70 miles south from their home in Galilee through Samaria to the other side of Jerusalem. Luke and Matthew put the birth in Judaea, at Bethlehem, because that was the city of David, and a Jewish king-messiah would naturally be descended from him: but John 7, 41f spoils Luke's story by telling us that some Jews said Jesus couldn't be the Messiah precisely because he came from Galilee and not from Bethlehem. (A.N. Wilson, *Jesus*, 74f, has a helpful discussion of the birth stories.)

When we sing 'While shepherds watched' we can either forget about history, and enjoy the ballad and what it teaches, in the best Christmas spirit, or concentrate on what really happened. The latter isn't going to do us or anyone around us much good, and it would be a great pity to renounce the carol. But we can enjoy it without pangs of intellectual conscience if we recognise its legendary quality: like most of the best stories, it is not unduly fact-bound.

From the mid-eighteenth century we have some fine Christmas hymns. *Adeste fideles* was written by a young English Catholic working at Douai in France, possibly as a

Jacobite rallying-song; it was Englished to 'O come, all ye faithful' in the next century. 'Hark the herald angels sing' was originally a hymn of the Incarnation by Charles Wesley starting 'Come, Desire of Nations, come,/ Fix in us thy humble home'; the Mendelssohn tune is of course later. 'Christians, awake' was written by John Byrom for his young daughter as a Christmas present, and its magnificent tune is contemporary. *NOBC* prints the whole poem of 52 lines, adding two lines to make up nine six-line stanzas, ending 'Saved by his Love, incessant we shall sing/ Of Angels and of Angel-men the King'. Even from the verses that survive in hymn-books we see that, rather in the manner of the old ballad-carols of the friars, we are taken past Christmas to the Crucifixion and to our chance of joyful redemption. From the singing of this hymn by friends under the Byroms' window at a minute past midnight came the old north-country custom - is it still alive? - of singing it in the street at midnight.

Hymns, including these hymn-carols, were beginning to become the sacred folk-song which the Wesleys soon made them, with a serious dogmatic purpose, often looking inward to the dialogue between Christ and the soul, rather than being ballad narratives of Mary and Joseph. By the mid-nineteenth century the Church of England had accepted the singing of hymns; collections of hymns with allocated tunes started (*Hymns Ancient and Modern* ran through many editions from 1861), and carols, which enthusiasts had started retrieving early in the century, gained wide circulation from the 1870s with the collection edited by Bramley and Stainer, both of Magdalen College, Oxford. By that time the observance of Christmas had begun to move towards what we can recognise; Prince Albert imported the Christmas tree from Germany, Dickens and others romanticised the winter snow; and Christmas cards began, with the (pagan?) holly, adding ivy for good measure. The Wise Men had long ago become Three Kings. The sentimentalisation of children, again following Dickens, will colour our response to the baby in the manger, and we may overlook what the old carols tell us about the hard realities of the baby's life.

On top of these additions to the Christmas story we pile Santa Claus, reindeer, Jingle Bells, and fire it all at Christmas shoppers from mobile loud-speakers so as to do our bit for charity. This is a long way from singing carols to express our joy and spread the news of the Birth.

Let us not neglect a fine hymn (by an American writer) which reminds us of world-wide sorrows and hopes: 'It came upon the midnight clear'. But is it enough to 'hear the angels sing', with nineteenth-century optimism, to bring about peace and the 'age of gold'?

Advent

Out of chronological order, let us glance at Advent, with its four Sundays before Christmas. Our approach to Christmas is deeper if we feel the whole sweep of the Christian year, opening with Advent. This is a solemn season, once kept as Lent is - the opposite of 'Only x shopping days to Christmas'. The Church traditionally prepares not only for Christ's birth but for his Second Coming (a concept which changed as the years wore on and nothing dramatic happened).

Advent is a season rich in hymns, expressing the wonder of Christ's birth, his redeeming sacrifice for mankind, and his coming again to judge and bring in the Kingdom of God. There can hardly be a better one than Charles Wesley's 'Lo! he comes with clouds descending', with its magnificent melody *Helmsley*, permeating and involving the singer and preparing us for the Christmas story. There are also translations of eighteenth-century Latin hymns ('O come, O come, Emmanuel' and 'On Jordan's bank'); Milton's 'The Lord will come and not be slow'; Wesley's 'Come, thou long-expected Jesus'; and (in a different vein, using the imagery of the Bridegroom's advent), the *Wachet auf* chorale, variously translated as 'Wake, O wake', 'Sleepers, wake', or 'Zion hears her watchmen's voices'.

Valuable motets are the settings by Palestrina and Byrd of *Rorate caeli desuper* (Isaiah 45, 8: Drop down, ye heavens, from above, and let the skies pour down righteousness: let the earth open, and let them bring forth salvation.) This, like many OT texts, is taken as anticipating Christian redemption, though it relates to the Jewish captivity in Babylon. Byrd sets the concluding *Gloria Patri* with a verve that recalls Monteverdi's 'Vespers of 1610' - written only three years later. Victoria's *Ecce Dominus veniet* is dramatic and very singable; at the other end of the dynamic range there is a charming anonymous fifteenth-century *Veni, veni Emmanuel* for two voices, probably nuns (ed. Mary Berry with English words: Schola Gregoriana of Cambridge, 1983).

Is it all 'Let's pretend'?

Some of us with a basically Puritan or scholarly conscience are likely to feel that the whole Christmas exercise is an immature sham; if believers in other religions sang words they did not believe, or perhaps even understand, we should deride it as mumbo-jumbo. Can we retrieve our integrity without losing the truth and joy of the belief handed down to us?

If we have any influence, we can try to avoid the carols/ hymns which are purely soft-centred. 'Silent Night' is, to me, one such; 'Away in a Manger' is another. This is deeply ingrained from childhood: but do we want to bring children up with what is an essentially sentimental picture? How do they later get away from it without complete disillusion? Is 'Once in royal David's city' right to encourage children to follow Christ by being 'Mild, obedient, good as he', when he was a rather headstrong child, developing into an uncompromising radical (see A.N. Wilson, 85f)? Are we hopelessly seduced by the magic of the solo boys in the King's College carols?

What we value in the Christmas story seems to differ widely. We know the nakedly commercial and materialistic emphasis on sales, consumption, expectations of gifts and their satisfaction; the hard-working parents who make a warm and welcoming home in which we can be sybaritic for a time; perhaps also the devout atmosphere of a church service which remembers, as medieval carols did, the height, depth, breadth of the Christian experience as we follow his life from Advent through Christmas to his sacrificial conquering of death. What we do about the words of the carols will depend on where the centre of our attention lies - on what god we follow - and on how much sentimental protection we demand against the pain of reality.

To write hymns or carols *for children* runs a great risk of writing down to them. Should we not concentrate on those that children can respond to, and which will last all their lives? Then it won't be automatic that they grow out of them or react against them at puberty. Any learned theology has to be in vivid form, as in some of the medieval and ballad carols like the 'Cherry Tree Carol' (*OBC* 66):

parents and ministers need to consider whether there something in the hard story of Jesus's life that we want to shield children from. And it is a rewarding exercise to go through the hymn-book critically, looking for those which do stand a chance of lasting through the child's life.

Familiarity is often the enemy of alertness; and we desensitise ourselves to the Christmas message of hope, sacrifice, acceptance and redemption if we habitually sing words without noticing them, or meaning them. This makes life less painful - and sometimes meaningless. (We are free to choose this way; there is an old saw, 'For those that like that kind of thing, that is the kind of thing they like'.)

Most of us will still want to join with our friends and neighbours and roar out the standard batch of carols and not bother too much about the precise meaning of the words. But then let's admit we are running on worn tyres that don't grip the surface. (What do the critical children think of this?) A re-tread means re-thinking what the words were meant to mean, and what they can mean for us. After a few Christmasses it may all sink in deeper.

9. HOLY WEEK AND EASTER

In Chapter 8 (pp. 103f) I touched on Advent, the solemn season which begins the Christian year, and I mentioned on pp. 96-9 that in the later Middle Ages Advent was a favourite season for carols instructing people in the whole of Christ's life. These gave a meaning to Christmas which went beyond the joyful winter festival and looked forward to the events at the end of Christ's life on earth, which the Church remembers in the week before Easter, Holy Week. Both Catholic and Lutheran services were richly endowed with music for this week. (To avoid interrupting these chapters with detail I am including in Appendix 1 short notes on the significance of important dates through the year.)

Palm Sunday

On the first day of Holy Week, Palm Sunday, Jesus rode into Jerusalem at a time when the Roman occupying forces were nervous of subversive disturbance. For the morning service English-speaking countries have fine settings, by Weelkes and Gibbons, of 'Hosanna to the Son of David'. There are two major hymns; 'All glory, laud and honour' is for a procession in which we re-enact the entry into the city, and it takes a cheerful view of the occasion. 'Ride on! ride on in majesty!', again with a fine seventeenth-century German tune (*Winchester New*), takes us more nearly to the heart of the matter. Jesus chose to make this formal entry, knowing that this was one of the stages to his death (indeed, his entry may have provoked the Romans to take action against him, to stop any possible Jewish revolt). He rode in on a donkey: 'In lowly pomp ride on to die'. This line almost passes before we can take it in. The last verse ends (and I regret the word 'meek' at this point) 'Bow thy meek head to mortal pain,/ Then take, O God, thy power and reign'. We are prepared for the events, later in the week, in which death is conquered through this divine sacrifice.

The singing of the 'Passion'

In the Catholic services on Palm Sunday and Good Friday the Gospel which tells of the Passion of Christ - his betrayal, trial and crucifixion - was intoned by the celebrant priest or the deacon, in Latin, and long before the Reformation it was in some places gradually dramatised. As a minimum, the deacon told the Evangelist's story, another priest sang the words of Christ, and a third (the 'Synagoga') sang the words of the maid, Peter, Pilate and the various groups or crowds of Jews, with a chorus of priests if there were enough.

The plainsong 'Passion' is a practical and effective way to present the Gospel with modest musical resources. There is an English version (deriving not from the original chant but from a sixteenth-century Roman recasting); this and the 'St John Passion' and other music for Holy Week was edited by Francis Burgess before the war for the now defunct Plainsong Publications Committee; some churches and libraries may have copies.

In the German Lutheran Church after the Reformation a rather different style gradually developed - the 'oratorio Passion', an extended setting in German with added devotional words, using either the normal musical resources of the church, including the enthusiastic singing of the congregation, or, as in Bach's Leipzig, a highly-trained choir and skilled instrumentalists. Schütz's 'St

Matthew Passion' is in the simpler style; it requires a good tenor as Evangelist, with other smaller solos and a chorus.

The Bach 'Passions'

Bach's 'St Matthew Passion' is a superb and massive work with sophisticated solo singing and orchestration, extended choruses as well as chorales; the English version at least is familiar to many singers and listeners. I venture the thought however that, particularly in listening to the meditative solos and chorales, the pain and remorse are too easily merely observed rather than being accepted. Let us remember the context: the Lutheran service divided an 'oratorio' *Passion* into two parts by the preaching of the sermon; and the chorales were hymns whose tunes and words were familiar to the congregation, who were free to join in singing them. All the other words, solo and chorus, were expected to be audible and comprehensible; the whole service became several hours long, and was an extended act of attentive devotion and of penitence. The music was an powerful instrument of the liturgy. A little book (*The Matthew Passion*) by John Fenton examines, in the context of Lenten devotions, the gospel text used by Bach, and a general introduction to the gospel is in his *St Matthew*, 9-23.

Bach's 'St John Passion' is immensely moving and very beautiful, and is not quite so large-scale a work. We all enjoy singing it, though it is hard work: but there are problems over the words. To begin with, whom do the chorus represent at any time? Then, if we are singing in German, some words are unfamiliar or archaic, and the frame of thought can be unexpected. This is often not conveyed by an edition in English, which provides bland singing translations. Choir trainers and soloists (at least) have to make or acquire literal translations. Appendix 2 makes suggestions on these points.

The German text can surprise us in its imagery. For instance, in 'Lie still', the long and devout final chorus (in C minor, with sarabande rhythm), the German words mean 'Enjoy peace, ye holy bones, which I now mourn no longer, and bring me - even me - to peace also. The grave which is appointed you [the bones], and which contains no more afflictions, opens my way to heaven, and shuts the gates of hell.' (But words in the English edition are undisturbing.) Then the final chorale, in Eb major, says (in the German) 'Ah Lord, when my life finishes let thy dear angel carry my spirit to Abraham's bosom, and let my corpse rest easy in its little bedroom, without care or torment, until the Last Day. Then awaken me from death, so that my eyes see thee in all joy, O Son of God, my Saviour and my throne of grace. Lord Jesus Christ, grant my prayer: I will glorify thee for ever.'

In their Gospels, on which the 'Passion' settings are built, Matthew and John each constructed a narrative which would illustrate his own understanding of Jesus. Matthew saw in him the Messiah (or Christ) who would lead the Jewish nation out of bondage and who would fulfil many OT prophecies; this would occur after the cataclysmic end of the world, within the lifetime of most of those then living; God's Judgment would separate those who would gain eternal life in the Kingdom of heaven from those to be cast aside for eternal punishment. John's view is different: the Kingdom was already present in Jesus, who was and is eternal life for those who believed in him ('I *am* the resurrection and the life'); this gift comes from God only if we have faith enough to give up the world, the past, even the community, for the new life. These concepts are explained in Fenton, *Finding the way through John*, 1-10, 140-4, and we come back to them on pp. 118f below.

Bach introduces into his 'St John Passion' two passages from St Matthew: the story (otherwise unattested) of the rending of the Temple veil and the earthquake in which the bodies of the saints arose; and (earlier) Peter's remorseful weeping. These additions are, if we may follow Pooh Bah in this solemn context, 'corroborative detail, intended to give artistic verisimilitude', making the text more dramatic and emotional. They change John's message by making it more grief-laden and apocalyptic.

Bach was following the example, and using part of the text, of a Passion oratorio of 1712 by B.H. Brockes, *Der Für die Sünde der Welt/ Gemarterte und Sterbende JESUS* ('Jesus, tortured and dying for the sins of the world'; *Deutsche Literatur ... in Entwicklungsreihen, Barock*, vol. 6, Leipzig, 1933). W. Flemming says (22f, my translation) 'Here Pilate or Judas sing dramatically and passionately, as formerly would only be heard from a hero on the [opera] stage. ... Especially the scourging and torture on the Cross are handled absolutely as they would be in a scene of torture and death in a drama'. This is helpful to us as singers, though it is not easy for us to approach.

Anti-semitism in the Passion narratives

Matthew and John were (with near-certainty) Jews who had responded to Christ's call; their angry depiction of the Jews, especially the Pharisees, in the Gospels was aimed at the majority who did not join them. Gentile Christians later absorbed the imputation of Jewish (rather than Roman) guilt for the death of Jesus; they may have been concerned to minimise persecution by keeping on the right side of the imperial power. But it led to hate by

Christians for the whole Jewish race, with the most terrible consequences: and this attitude has only been formally rescinded by the Roman Catholic Church in recent years, by a change of heart in the Vatican.

Should we, then, censor or put aside the great settings of the 'Passion'? Are we helping to perpetuate a misguided and potentially poisonous attitude which can cause genuine offence and hurt? There is, unusually, a genuine case here for 'political correctness': but I do not believe we should distort or forgo some of the greatest musical works of all time. One solution is suggested to me by remembering several Good Friday mornings when a group of us met in a magnificent but cold church on a hill in Warwickshire to sing the English version of the plainsong 'St John Passion' (p. 108 above). We rehearsed the crowd choruses with whoever would come and sing, working briefly on each until it was strong and vivid and we could respond to the events being told by the three soloists. As we did this it seemed to us that *we* were calling for Christ's death, and that the guilt was with our own betrayal.

In preparing Bach's 'Passion' chorales, with their guilt-stricken meditations, choirs and their directors might consider thinking of our present responsibilities, even though we are singing about the Jews of first-century Palestine. Matthew was himself a Jew, but a pro-Roman and anti-Jewish bias affects particularly his account of Pilate's attitude at the trial. There is no way of 'fudging' this point in Bach's 'St Matthew Passion'; it is part of the structure, and all we can do is to put the point to our audiences in a programme note or, for a liturgical performance, the sermon. (A further instance of anti-semitism, in a medieval motet, is discussed on pp. 130f.)

John Donne's Sonnet XI faces the temptation towards anti-semitism; here is his massive first octave:

Spit in my face you Jewes, and pierce my side,
Buffet, and scoffe, scourge, and crucifie mee,
For I have sinn'd, and sinn'd, and onely hee,
Who could do no iniquitie, hath dyed:
But by my death can not be satisfied
My sinnes, which passe the Jewes impiety:
They kill'd once an inglorious man, but I
Crucifie him daily, being now glorified.

The Protestant Good Friday

Now, as in Bach's time, St Matthew's Gospel is customarily heard on Palm Sunday, and St John's on Good Friday (though concert performances of the big oratorio *Passions* may not follow this pattern). Other works include two old non-liturgical favourites, Maunder's 'Olivet to Calvary' and Stainer's 'Crucifixion' (which I do not know well enough to offer comment). The Schütz 'Seven Words from the Cross' (in English or German), with organ or strings, is grave and effective and not difficult; and there is an odd little compilation of his 'Passion Music' (Novello) for accompanied four-part choir, low tenor Evangelist and bass Jesus, which looks useful for amateur choirs.

Tenebrae

For the days immediately before Easter the Catholic services which may involve music are principally those for the three days of the 'triduum', Maundy Thursday (the night of the agony in Gethsemane), Good Friday (the crucifixion and burial) and Holy Saturday (during which Christ lay in the tomb). The outstanding works are many settings of the 'Lamentations of Jeremiah' (by Tallis, White,

Byrd, A. Ferrabosco II among Tudor composers), and of the Responds by Victoria and Ingegneri. 'Tenebrae' (darkness) is the name for Matins (which was a night service) during the triduum. The service, in both monastic and 'secular' churches, includes three 'nocturns', each of which has three (sometimes four) sets of lessons from the 'Lamentations of Jeremiah', followed by responds (or 'responsories'). These are short refrains, often from the Gospels, sung before and after a verse of a psalm; Victoria's set of eighteen moving and beautiful settings has been edited for Chesters by Bruno Turner. For each of the three days of the triduum the first nocturn has Victoria's polyphonic 'Lamentations' followed by chanted responsories, and in the second and third nocturns the lessons are chanted and the responsories are polyphonic.

The Hebrew texts of the lessons are acrostic poems where the initial letters of the verses are in alphabetical succession; the Greek and Latin texts took over these Hebrew letters as headings. In the polyphonic settings of the 'Lamentations' composers treated these letters as if they were illuminations in a manuscript. The biblical text laments the exile of the Jews, the condition of their homeland (the first Temple was destroyed by the Babylonians in 586 BC), and the frame of mind of those who were still there; it ends with a call to Jerusalem, and thus to the Jewish nation, *Convertere ad dominum tuum* - 'turn again to thy God' (taken from Hosea 14). The text of these OT lessons, at first sight inappropriate for a time so close to the centre of the Christian story, agrees with the desolation of the disciples in those days: and the acceptance of the need - though hardly yet the hope - of redemption and rebirth.

These are powerful and emotional texts, and I find that nearly everyone enjoys singing Tallis's setting: but the same note of caution is needed as with hymns and the Bach 'Passions' - we can too easily sing about these painful and desperate events in a semi-detached manner, or else sentimentally (with emotion that is shallow, or even self-indulgent). By the end, something in us should have changed, whether we are singing for ourselves privately or as part of the liturgy.

The sacred music-dramas

At some great churches, notably in the monastery at Fleury and at Winchester, short dramas were sung for various occasions of the year, with some sort of costume and rubrics for movement or gesture. For the Resurrection there is the medieval music-drama, *Visitatio sepulchris* (in Latin or English), with the three Marys. To the narrative chant were added hymns such as the eleventh-century *Victimae paschali*; and the Easter play would end with the *Te Deum*, in grand procession. (The somewhat later 'Mystery plays', surviving in midland and northern English dialects, were very popular and involved the townspeople and gilds in acting, speaking and singing; the plays were not part of the liturgy.)

Easter

Polyphonic motets on the beginning of Easter Day include Taverner's and Tallis's settings of Luke's account of the women who brought spices to the tomb, *Dum transisset Sabbatum*, based on a plainsong melody; Morley's *Eheu sustulerunt Dominum* (Mary Magdalene to Peter, 'They have taken away my Lord out of the sepulchre, and we know not where they have laid him': John 20, 2). On the

Resurrection we have Tye's 'Christ rising again' (a good noisy way to occupy six parts including divided tenors and basses) and Gibbons's 'I am the resurrection and the life', but neither is very distinguished. Schütz's 'Resurrection Story' (German or English) divides the choir into six, then eight, easy parts, with simple solos and four violas da gamba or the equivalent. And there are several well-known and joyful hymns, and a major oratorio by Elgar, 'The Apostles' (second part).

But Easter, the greatest festival of the Church, has not brought the flood of great and rich liturgical music that we might have expected, and it is not easy to suggest exactly why: perhaps composers find suffering easier to experience, and re-create, than the mystery and joy of the resurrection. (Beethoven takes us a long way, without words, in the last quartets.)

One of the most powerful pieces of Easter music is non-liturgical - Part III of Handel's 'Messiah'. We have heard the great statement by the soprano, in the bright key of E major:

For now is Christ risen from the dead, the first-fruits of them that sleep.

Then suddenly unaccompanied and with anguished harmony in A minor, the chorus sings:

Since by man came death,

and answers itself in C major, with full orchestra,

by man came also the resurrection of the dead.

And similarly, in G minor followed by a brisk D minor,

For as in Adam all die,
    even so in Christ shall all be made alive.
        (1 Corinthians 15, 20-22)

We are back to a favourite carol and hymn subject: sinful man as the first Adam, redeemed through the opportunity given by Christ, the second Adam (pp. 96f). The scale and colouring of Handel's version makes this short section a dramatic experience for the singers (unless they are deaf to the words) and for the audience. We are ready to hear about the mystery and the last trumpet.

And trumpets make *Et resurrexit* in Bach's Mass in B minor into one of life's unforgettable experiences. These words are of course, to our eternal good fortune, not just for Easter but, if we wish it, for every day.

The Mystery and the Gospel

This is an impossible section to write, but I must try. In Chapters 4 and 6 I set out what we understand that orthodox believers hoped and feared in past centuries, and this will apply also to many people today. How may the singer of today and his friends, if not steeped in traditional religious belief, interpret the evidently all-important beliefs about death and resurrection?

Harry Williams, in *True Resurrection* (5, 8) forthrightly asks why resurrection means little to us for most of the time; 'what interest can people be expected to take in fantasies of life beyond the grave which look as if they are little more than wishful thinking?' This certainly troubles me. I can see the possibility that after the death of a body an element of personal consciousness may persist, perhaps for only a short time; such occurrences have long been the subject of serious psychical research. I imagine that an unquiet spirit which haunts and wanders until it finds its rest or its end finds its experience frustrating rather than beatific: but I am told that someone who has been very close to a dead person may feel a sense of warmth and benevolence for a time. For myself I have no objection, once I die, to ceasing to exist: what happens in life is what matters, while we have our powers of action and enjoyment. (I mention Hamlet's views on the matter on pp. 37f.)

The confusion arises not only from centuries of orthodox teaching about eternal (or everlasting) life. A continuation, in a heaven above the sky, of the present life but without its suffering was, like Hell, an idea designed for simple folk; I mentioned on pp. 38f that theologians realised this in the early centuries AD, but it came generally to be taken literally.) Many of Jesus's immediate followers, particularly Matthew, had expected the end of the world during their lifetime. Christ would then come in glory, and God would rule in his Kingdom for ever, so those who at the Last Judgment gained entry to the kingdom would have eternal life. But on one important point Matthew and his friends were wrong: the apocalyptic end of the world didn't happen. They went on expecting it for some decades at least, and the original idea of the nature of eternal life gradually lost its force.

In John's Gospel however (see *Finding the way through John*, especially 6, 9, 65, 143), the coming of Christ (the Messiah) is not an event in the apocalyptic future, but it is already present in the life of Jesus, who is the Son of God, bringing salvation to the Jews and in our lives. To those who have been chosen to believe, and who respond by giving up their old lives to follow him, Jesus manifests himself as their life, light and salvation: and this means now, not after death. But some are overcome by the darkness, and do not receive the gift that he offers; Jesus answered the Jews, apparently harshly, at the feast of the dedication (John 10, 25-7):

... I told you, and ye believed not because ye are not of my sheep.... My sheep hear my voice, and I know them, and they follow me.

Changing the focus so that redemption and eternal life relate to our lives on earth means facing the offer of resurrection now; there is less time than when we are thinking about what might happen after death. We are back to Harry Williams's book, which explains resurrection as a source of support, direction and vitality of unexpected power. On p. 12f he says that the presence with us of Jesus, the creative Word (see p. 51 above), makes us fully alive, in body and mind. I become a person in resurrection, and the agent of goodness; and Williams continues:

all that separates and injures and destroys is being overcome by what unites and heals and creates.

I suggest that these thoughts are a key to dissolving two of today's disorders: the feelings of absence of identity, and a lack of meaning in life.

Suffering, death, and redemption

Suffering and death are part of our lives as well as vitality and joy. For Christ they were an inevitable part of the life which ended with the conquest of death in the cataclysmic events of Good Friday and Easter - whatever it was that physically happened in that physical and spiritual darkness. Paul explained this doctrine of 'atonement' to the Romans and the Corinthians (cf. pp. 96f, 117) in terms of Adam's fall and the Second Adam, but John, writing many years later, puts it differently. Early in John's Gospel (1, 29), John the Baptist hailed Jesus before baptising him, 'Behold the Lamb of God, which taketh away the sin of the world'. Jesus took past and future sins and sufferings on himself, once and for all, to give his followers the chance of redemption - of resurrection. That *qui tollis peccata mundi* is what gives the believer confidence to pray *dona nobis pacem*. And these words in the *Agnus Dei* are part of every Mass, including every Requiem, and have inspired sublime music; perhaps composers have been more able to respond to resurrection when it has been transmuted into a personal hope than when confronted with the mystery of Easter itself.

On death and resurrection Harry Williams writes (151), in a passage not unworthy of St Paul,

If suffering by means of its very death-dealing qualities can be life-giving, that is because in our suffering the Eternal Word is made flesh, and that silent presence never ceases to create us in the moment where the First Day and the Last Day are one and the same. As dying and behold we live, as having nothing and yet possessing all things, that is life eternal here now.

And he puts death in the perspective of resurrected life (180):

If we are ready for life in the sense of being open to its power and possibilities, then we are also ready for death. If we are aware of resurrection in the present, then we shall not be over-concerned about resurrection in the future.

I have felt myself to be a heretic on several points of orthodox doctrine, and the eager expectation of life after death is one such. I was therefore delighted to hear in my church a sermon by a very eminent theologian, Dr John Macquarrie, lately Lady Margaret Professor of Divinity at Oxford University and Canon of Christ Church. I think that it will be helpful to readers of this book to have its text (Appendix 3); I am grateful for the necessary permission. Readers may also find helpful his *Jesus Christ in Modern Thought*; on pp. 400-14 he approaches these mysteries of Christ's death and resurrection in two ways, the conventional 'happy ending' and a more austere ending which follows St John. He suggests that Christ's victory over evil was already won in the agonising hours before his death, and that it would remain decisive even if there were no subsequent events. (For many believers, however, the decisive and central event is the historical and physical Resurrection.)

10. OUR INTEGRITY AS SINGERS

We come full circle to the question in Chapter 1 - 'why do we sing?' - and add 'how do we sing?' I have used the word 'integrity' because we need to be honest about whether or not our real persons are playing a full part in our singing. There is a range of possibilities. If I am to be Herod in a medieval *mystery play*, there is a venerable tradition and expectation that I shall 'ham it' unmercifully. (The same expectation arises, probably via the Commedia dell'Arte, in *pantomime*.)

In a more sophisticated manner, a staged *opera* demands that we leave our own characters and grow, or jump, into the thoughts and emotions of a person created by the author and fleshed out by the composer. We convey the meaning of the words-and-music to the audience using uninhibitedly the whole range of vocal expression, timing, gesture and movement that the style of the particular opera allows - statuesque, flamboyant or romantically demonstrative. While we do this we ourselves are hidden behind - protected by? - the mask of the stage character; we are presenting someone else and not ourselves.

If instead we are singing *Lieder* (which are outside the scope of this book) we have to project the poet's voice (whether or not he uses a character to speak his words) within a style and convention which is far more limited - we must use voice and eyes, no gesture or movement.

Where do we stand on *oratorio*? This affects solo singers particularly; I understand that they often feel that they are naked without the protection given by stage character, costume and make-up. The conventions are close to those for *Lieder*, but have to be mantained in the face of a big audience, an orchestra and a conductor.

In all these ways of singing, the composer and we have the same understanding of the way singers approach the music. But for *liturgical music* we need to pause and consider. In a cathedral-type or college choir a well-established tradition leads one to sing, say, Stanford in Bb with expression and enjoyment, but without attempting to impersonate Mary and Simeon in the *Magnificat* and *Nunc dimittis*. Instead, their words have rather awkwardly become ours, coloured by our reaction to the Lord who has scattered the proud; and we, like Simeon, have seen the salvation which came with the incarnation of God in Jesus, to be a light to lighten the Gentiles (us). Stanford, working in that same collegiate environment, will hardly have expected his choir to convey to the congregation much beyond decently enthusiastic Anglican devotion.

Lutheran music

If we sing a Bach *chorale* a gap opens. 'O sacred head, sore wounded' may take us beyond the limits of our own religious feeling. The seventeenth-century German Pietist translator of a penitential medieval Latin lyric makes us sing, in the English version' 'In thy most bitter passion/ My heart to share doth cry,/ With thee for my salvation/ Upon the cross to die.' I am not sure that if my heart really cried to die in this way, I should be capable of singing about it: so can I avoid insincerity?

For Lutherans of that time, these words must have been more highly charged than our natural style of worship makes them; perhaps for many, sympathetic with Pietist verse, the response was highly emotional: others may just have felt more guilty and inadequate. Before we in the late twentieth century can do anything but skate over the text, we have to jerk ourselves into an age of early death and fear of Hell. If we then find something we value in the words-and-music, we need to communicate strongly with our hearers. If we are singing liturgically, this may - should? - affect the whole course of the service.

Soloists in the Bach 'Passions' will find even more self-indulgent texts; does one take an operatic (or even a *Lieder* singer's) attitude to these, abstracting from one's own personal response? The 'Passion' is not poetic fiction like opera or lieder. Singing Peter or Pilate demands impersonation: but a meditative aria, whose text is not taken from the Gospel, is sung on behalf of all those present. In 'Gladly would I take upon me Cross and Cup, and all His burden, Could I follow Christ my Lord' ('St Matthew Passion', no. 29, in Sir Ivor Atkins's careful English version), for whom is the bass soloist speaking these terrible words? For himself, on our behalf? It is easiest for us as singers to impute this resolve merely to a character whom the far-away author may have had in mind - the faithful soul, or the Daughter of Zion. But is this good enough, and is it what Bach intended?

Even the chorus, singing the German text rather than a sanitised English translation, has in the 'St John Passion' a chorale (no. 52) which may be literally translated as 'For comfort in my own need, may I see the image of thee, my kindest Lord Christ, bleeding to death'. My own reaction is that this feels a contorted and masochistic religion. But the more we skate over it, the less of the great musical work we are giving. When we see paintings with a similar agonised theme - the Grünewald altarpiece at Colmar is an obvious example - we can stand and look for a long time, and walk away in silence, changed or unchanged. But singing the words, especially to an audience or congregation, is a challenge that does not allow silence.

We sometimes have confusing switches of role, as in the *St John Passion* choruses. In Annex 2 (p. 144) I have thought it useful to set out this succession of roles; it is clear from the music that Bach wanted some of them strongly characterised - and one must decide how to deal with the anti-Jewish overtones.

Catholic music

Here let us work backwards in time. Much routine Catholic music of the last century or so has a content and accepted style which may be too trivial or sentimental for many of us. Pius X complained in 1903 about the abuse of Vespers:

Instead of the pious chanting of the clergy, in which the faithful too could take part, endless musical compositions on the words of the Psalms have been substituted, formed in the style of the old theatrical works, most of them of such small value as works of art that they would not be borne even in second-rate secular concerts.

However vivid this music may have sounded in the mouths of uncritical and faithful people, it was too much for Pope Pius, who in his reforming *Motu proprio* forbade all but Gregorian chant and simple polyphony of the Palestrina school (his text is given in *Singing in Latin*, 301-5). The concerted music he complained of is still performed, in some churches and in concerts; especially eighteenth-century Masses by Haydn and Mozart, where despite the beauty of the music the treatment of words is often ornate or (when there are many words in the liturgical text) abbreviated and trivial. Perhaps one can best sing this as frankly quasi-operatic music, especially as many contemporary church soloists at the time were principally opera singers.

But let us look at what composers were saying around 1600 about writing and singing religious music. In 1605 Byrd published his first volume of *Gradualia*, motets for the Church's year. In the Latin dedication to his friend Henry Howard, Earl of Northampton and son of the poet Surrey, he comments on the beauty of the words which he has set to music; the words themselves have inspired him, for (in the translation by E.H. Fellowes in his *William Byrd*),

there is a certain hidden power ... in the thoughts underlying the words themselves; so that, as one meditates upon the sacred words and constantly and seriously considers them, the right notes, in some inexplicable manner, suggest themselves quite spontaneously.

The composer is an important 'factor of production' in the ecclesiastical music industry, but not the only one. In 1597 Thomas Morley (*A Plain and Easy Introduction to Practical Music*, 1952 edn., 292f) wrote that a motet

made on a ditty requireth most art and moveth and causeth most strange effects in the hearer, being aptly framed for the ditty and well expressed by the singer, for it will draw the auditor (and specially the skilful auditor) into a devout and reverent kind of consideration of Him for whose praise it was made. ... the matter is now come to that state that though a song be never so well made and never so aptly applied to the words yet shall you hardly find singers to express it as it ought to be, for most of our churchmen, so they can cry louder in their choir than their fellows, care for no more, whereas by the contrary they ought to study how to vowel and sing clean, expressing their words with devotion and passion whereby to draw the hearer, as it were, in chains of gold by the ears to the consideration of holy things.

Perhaps Byrd, with his secret services sung by a devout few, was less troubled by insensitive singers than Morley at Old St Paul's - we can note that some of our present discontents are not new! Byrd was deeply moved by the religious struggles of his Church, and we in turn are attracted and moved by his strong feeling for the words, so skilfully expressed: but only a Roman Catholic can fully and genuinely express what Byrd wrote. Protestants and non-believers can enjoy singing his motet 'Turn our captivity, O Lord, as a brook in the South. They that sow in tears shall reap in joyfulness.' But it wasn't our captivity, and what the Catholic rulers led by Philip of Spain were attempting to achieve, through the infiltrated Jesuits, was the restoration of the Roman Church in England. The author of Ps. 126, from which Byrd took the text, was of course not concerned with the English Catholics but with the captivity of Zion (that is, the Chosen People) in Babylon 2000 years earlier, and the music may well speak to other oppressed people. We from our safe distance can sing it with a certain sympathy: but even if we try to impersonate, as an actor would, it can hardly have the edge of passion and near-despair of Catholics under persecution.

Counter-reformation and Renaissance

In the late fifteenth century, a century before Byrd and well before the insistence of the counter-reformation and the Council of Trent that the (Latin) words should be clearly heard, there was a change in the attitude of composers to word-setting. This followed the revelation by humanist scholars of the beauty and expressiveness of classical poetry, and their new emphasis on the ancient art of rhetoric. Dante, Boccaccio and Petrarch had earlier shown the expressiveness of words in the new Italian language. The mature works of Josquin led his contemporaries and then Lassus and Monteverdi into the rich world of word-expression which we have now come to take for granted. Rhetoric again was important for Willaert when from his influential position at St Mark's, Venice, he showed how music and words had greater power - greater *affect* - when their accentuation was mutually consistent. (The humanists argued in terms of 'length' of syllable, which is what is relevant to classical quantitative verse, but they muddled this with stress accentuation, which can lie on a 'short' syllable. It is the unstressed, rather than the short, syllable on which Willaert generally avoids a melisma; this system has become familiar to us through its adoption by Palestrina and most later composers.)

The three formal levels of rhetoric, the humanists taught, should be observed by composers and by singers: *gravis*, to move the hearer by eloquence or elegance; *mediocris*, to entertain pleasantly, and *humilis*, the straightforward approach suitable for teaching. Music and poetry, the humanists said, should be rejoined; they been one unified art in classical Greece but had developed separately through the Middle Ages. The styles of singing Renaissance music depend on these ideas: a full discussion is in D. Harrán, *In Search of Harmony.*

The Late Middle Ages

Before then we have less guidance on the *colouring* of our singing - or even the precise notes to be sung. There is every reason to suppose that composers, who were often also directors of choirs, chose their adult singers for the quality of their singing and not just for its accuracy or loudness. But musicality and technical training were needed too. The singer had a manuscript, often newly written, for his own part only. He had to interpret the rhythmic notation - note-lengths depended on their context within the phrase; the composer often left him to decide how to underlay the words; and he had to apply rules and musical discretion on questions of pitch, since he was often not told, for instance, what sort of F to sing (what we should call F# or not). All this required intense listening to what other parts were singing, and thus to the music as a whole. Modern performers, even highly expert groups, commonly use modern transcriptions, and may be too dependent on what an editor has decided, and need to be used to singing from facsimile single parts (Margaret Bent, 'Editing early music: the dilemma of translation', *Early Music*, August 1994, 373-92).

In liturgical chant there will sometimes be a phrase in the written music which suggests that the (unknown) composer is reacting to the *meaning* of the Latin text, and this can hardly be sung completely deadpan. But the underlying attitude was that the words spoke for themselves; that the singer was part of a collective act of worship, not an individual expressing his reaction to the holy scriptures or to God's works. The words were addressed to God, and not to a congregation in need of persuasion. All this applies to chant of any date, and it may be a useful guide for pre-1500 polyphony also. Modern singers, used to later music, can fall into a romantic and individualistic style which would not at that time have been tolerable: but singing had purpose and conviction.

There is a minefield in certain motets - the hidden references and hermetic symbols, mathematical, political, religious or personal. An example is given by Paula Higgins (*Early Music*, November 1994, 710). In Busnoys's *Anima mea liquefacta est* the meanings (concealed in liturgically appropriate texts), though ostensibly devotional, convey to those who are 'in the know' an astonishing variety of extra-devotional meanings and symbols centred on court events in 1445-6. If the uninstructed singer meets such a text, his artistic integrity may not be at risk, but he will be missing the point, which was directed to a sophisticated and informed few. Most of us will fall far short of interpreting the more obscure passages; one needs (for instance) a Busnoys expert, or a medieval Latinist who knows the detailed historical background.

Anti-semitism in the text

In medieval hymns or motets we may come across unpalatable attitudes like the anti-semitism in the *Passions* (and in the Gospels themselves); I called attention to this on pp. 111-3. Richard Taruskin (*Text and Act*, 357) challenges the assumption that the 'artistic integrity' of a work is all that matters. He quotes a recording of Busnoys's *Victimae Paschali*, the sixth verse of which means 'More trust is to be put in honest Mary alone than in the lying crowd of Jews'. This comes from an eleventh-century Easter Sequence which rests on the account in Matthew 28 of Mary Magdalene's visit to the tomb, and of a story, spread through bribery by the Jewish authorities, that Christ's body had been stolen by the disciples; 'and this saying is commonly reported among the Jews until this day' (Matthew 28, 15). Taruskin points out that the text was left out of the Catholic liturgy long ago; need it be included in a modern performance? He is concerned, I think, with the effect on hearers. I want to ask also what is in the singer's mind. Does he notice? If so, should he be cynically or clinically professional, or should he 'ham it'? The offending verse is part of a through-composed structure; one cannot just omit it and preserve the full version in the library. Taruskin suggests vocalising or bowdlerising by substituting for *Judeorum* the word *peccatorum* (which is an ugly side-step, though it could suggest our own involvement in the betrayal - see p. 112 above). Clearly there are other things in life than insistence on one particular element of 'authenticity'. But of course any textual change should be noted for the listener.

Involvement

Let us return to the normal run of pre-Reformation music, before humanist enthusiasm for rhetoric affected composers and singers. When we attempt its re-creation, we should of course avoid anachronistic romanticism, but at the same time our singing has to be convinced and involved. Continental listeners sometimes find our excellent small choirs too cool and detached. What may be behind this? Four or five hundred years ago the singer of polyphonic music, or of chant, was a cog in the whole liturgical scene, which (as I have mentioned on p. 31) involved much more than the music and the words - vestments, gesture and movement, incense, bells. In a monastery all the participants would be known to each other and share a common discipline and dedication. In a great collegiate church or cathedral there might be a great crowd of townspeople standing in the nave for the Mass. The singers often worked alongside the composer, or were directed by him. The whole of the lives from which the music sprang was different from ours; their musical experience was deep and closely focussed, though far narrower than ours. Works which to us are both venerable and familiar were to them new, modern, music.

Singers and congregations then were affirming a faith - their own faith; and from the 1530s this was violently opposed to the new Protestantism that most of us have inherited. Holding to a prescribed faith was obligatory not only in Catholic countries but in those holding to Lutheran or Calvinist Protestantism. As a result of political struggles and the change of intellectual climate with the eighteenth-century Enlightenment we have also inherited the freedom not to accept any precise belief; part of our difficulty in gaining a satisfactory relationship to late medieval music lies in this very freedom, and the allied duty to think and decide for oneself.

To the Protestant, worship is centred in expressing one's personal response to God and his creation: but the medieval choirman was performing an office which was to be offered to God before the people, or one's colleagues, and which was effective in its own right without the expression of personal emotion - though deep emotion may often have been felt. What mattered was not the individual's personal response but the discipline of observance by all present. This must affect the style that we judge to be appropriate when singing their music: the age of romantic sensibility had not yet come.

We are, I think, without much documentary evidence to give us positive guidance, though we know that in the twelfth century Abbot Ailred of Rievaulx frowned on chanters who gesticulated, grimaced during the sacred offices, or imitated thunder, women's voices or horses neighing (*OBC*, viii). But if this be offence, does any choir remains innocent after singing the refrain in Ps. 18, v. 12f? It must surely be enjoyed:

At the brightness of his presence his clouds removed:
      hailstones and coals of fire.
The Lord also thundered out of heaven, and the Highest gave his thunder:
      hailstones, and coals of fire.

That is an easy case, because the *Book of Common Prayer*, from which the Psalms are customarily sung, is alive with us still (if sadly neglected). When we move into Catholic Latin or Middle English, or Lutheran German, we can only try to develop a sympathy from what we can find out about the religious and artistic outlook of singers and worshippers of that time and place. This involves not only study but a disturbing use of our imagination, such as perhaps the discipline and training of the best actors or poetry-readers attain.

Even when we manage this, we are singing not as a part of the liturgy which was at the centre of the professional lives of the choirs of the times, surrounded by clerical colleagues, but to a modern audience or (rarely) congregation. Our experience, and their reaction, must be different from those of 500 years ago. We have to be deeply involved but to be conscious of the need for artificial adaptation to whatever our surroundings are - Holywell Music Room, Royal Albert Hall or Brompton Oratory. (If we sing for mechanical reproduction we can't know who we are singing to, and this inevitably removes us still further from the record companies' rainbow-end of 'authenticity'.)

Who should sing?

How far, indeed, does singing religious music, of any period, require in us adherence to the relevant faith? To be ultra-purist might lead to a doctrine of 'religious correctness' where a soloist in a Bach 'Passion' had to be a Lutheran, and in a Mozart Mass a Roman Catholic, and most people would wish to avoid such a system of ghetto music wherever possible. Beethoven's 'Mass in D', though intended for his friend Archduke Rudolf's installation as Archbishop, was not used liturgically; Verdi's *Requiem* was specifically not so intended; most other religious works were written for the liturgy or for private devotion.

For concert performances I suggest two tests: the singer must respond thoroughly to the music (which carries the words, and in music of the last few hundred years may be strongly affected by them); and he should not be out of sympathy with the religious intent of the work. The necessary act of presenting the work persuasively will then be possible, if sometimes difficult. Perhaps singers of the appropriate faith, race and language will have a perceptibly different quality: but the rest of us can try with a clear conscience, and may even manage a less parochial view of the music itself. But if the occasion is liturgical or devotional, we have to think again.

Think for a moment of another end of the musical world, the political or nationalist song. Many but not all of us, if we were offered money, would make a reasonable shot at singing the Nazi marching song, the *Horst-Wessel-Lied*, for a radio play. But suppose a newspaper magnate started a Fascist movement here, and engaged a choir for a mass rally: nearly all of us would refuse. The use of the singing would be morally poisonous, and the intended reactions of the audience unrestrainedly evil.

And although at the last night of the Proms we may stretch a point by joining in 'Rule Britannia', led by an eminent mezzo in fancy dress, we might hesitate to help out with the last night of someone else's party conference. Similarly in religious music: for concert performance I have suggested we need full sympathy with the music, and no antipathy to words and doctrine, but in a liturgical or devotional context we need a strong actual sympathy with the words and doctrine, even if not actual adherence to the relevant creed, before we agree to sing - or indeed before we are asked to sing.

Envoi - I

I have been urging readers to do things which I am sure I cannot manage properly myself - to take seriously what we sing, and to follow through the promptings of our moral, artistic and scholarly consciences. That is all terribly obvious, though unfashionable, but perhaps it is time someone put up a marker!

Envoi - II

A friend reading this book tells me that it is terribly English, and would not fit the U.S. market. I plead guilty; it has seemed important to write of what I know and feel, and to have in mind the singers I know. It would be spoilt if I tried, without much experience of the States, to introduce mid-Atlantic language and attitudes, but I hope someone will write a book which is more suitable for American eyes.

APPENDIX 1 :
THE ECCLESIASTICAL YEAR

I outlined on pp. 34-7 the medieval calendar of the Western Church. I will now list the main dates in the Church's Year, in the traditional form - that is, as in the Catholic tradition before and after the reforms of the Council of Trent (promulgated in 1564) and in the *Book of Common Prayer* (from 1549). Other saints' days generally observed are listed in John Harper, *The Forms and Orders of Western Liturgy*, 237-41; he also lists those which in the Medieval and Tridentine rites were included in the *Temporale* and those in the *Sanctorale*. Some of the celebrations were subject to centuries of controversy: see the relevant entries in *ODCC* and, for the complex early history of the principal festivals, T.J. Talley, *The Origins of the Liturgical Year*.

Some seasons and feasts relate to the *solar calendar*, and do not vary from year to year. This takes over pagan and Roman celebrations of the winter solstice and the vernal equinox. There is, however, a complication: when Julius Caesar introduced this calendar in BC 46 his year lasted for 365¼ days instead of 365.2422. In this he may be forgiven, but by AD 325 the error meant that the vernal equinox occurred on 21 March instead of 25 March, and it was the former which entered into the calculation of the date of Easter agreed at the Council of Nicaea. Gregory XIII corrected the Julian calendar as used in the Roman Catholic Church by omitting ten days from 1582; in 1752 his calendar was adopted also in England, by when one more day had to be lost: the popular cry was 'Give us back our

Eleven Days'. The present arrangement for leap years only needs correction about every 3000 years.

Other seasons depend on the *lunar calendar*. The first day of the Jewish Passover (see p. 11) is celebrated at the first full moon after the spring equinox (for this purpose 21 March), and the Christian Pasch, now 'Easter', is in the Western Church on the following Sunday. The latest possible date on this system is 25 April.

The lunar year, with thirteen months of 27.32 days (about 2/3 of a day shorter than the conventional 28), is about ten days shorter than a solar year. So if Easter has been late in Year 0, the Passover and Easter (Paschal) full moon will occur about ten days earlier in Year 1 (about eleven in a Leap Year). The same for Year 2; but if we do this again in Year 3 the date will usually come before 21 March, in which case we must take the full moon of a later lunar month; Easter will then be about eighteen days later than in Year 2.

The Orthodox Church follows the (uncorrected) Julian Calendar, explained above, and Easter may therefore be later.

The date of Easter was one of the main differences between the Celtic and Roman Churches in Britain; the Synod of Whitby (664) decided in favour of the Roman, Julian, system.

Chapter 4 (p. 36f) described this duple succession of feasts. List A gives the principal feasts of the solar calendar, and List B those depending on the lunar calendar. I have followed Harper's list in showing in capitals the principal feasts, and solemn days in Holy Week.

I add to these lists a few seasonal anthems and motets; for Advent and Christmas see Chapter 8, and for Holy

Week and Easter Chapter 9. Marian antiphons are shown according to their modern usage.

Byrd's *Gradualia* contains settings, for the main feasts of the year, of the Proper of the Mass - that is, the seasonal liturgy which was set to music to complement the unchanging items, the Ordinary. (A new edition of *Gradualia* has been issued by JOED Music Publications, 234 Stanley Park Road, Carshalton Beeches, SM5 3JP; fifteen of the twenty volumes contain music for specific feasts.) There is an earlier set of Propers, basing the polyphony on Gregorian chant melodies, by Isaac (*Choralis constantinus*, 1507-9). It was completed by his pupil Senfl and published 1550-5; modern edns. in three volumes, Vienna 1898 and 1909, Ann Arbor, 1950. Sets of Offertories (but not the rest of the Proper) were written by Lassus (*c.*1580) and Palestrina (1585: Kalmus/ Casimiri edn., and Gregg Press, Ridgewood, New Jersey).

LIST A: **Solar calendar.**

Advent	Begins on the first day of the Church's year, the fourth Sunday before Christmas. (*ASB* year starts with nine Sundays before Christmas.) Marian antiphon (until 2 Feb.), *Alma redemptoris mater*.
St Andrew	30 November (may fall before Advent).
CONCEPTION of the BVM	8 December (Immaculate Conception).
CHRISTMAS	25 December.
St Stephen, first martyr	26 December.
St John the Apostle	27 December.
Holy Innocents	28 December (Herod's slaughter of the male infants, as in 'Coventry Carol'; *Vox in Rama*).
St Thomas of Canterbury	29 December.
Circumcision	1 January.
EPIPHANY	6 January (Manifestation of Christ to the Gentiles in the persons of the Magi; also Baptism of Christ; and Miracle at Cana). Marenzio's *Tribus miraculis* covers these three celebrations, Palestrina's magnificent *Surge, illuminare*, à 4+4, and Byrd's, à 4, only the first. See note at end on Sundays after Epiphany.
Conversion of St Paul	25 January.

PURIFICATION of the
    Blessed Virgin Mary   2 February (Candlemas;
Presentation of Christ in the
Temple: Byrd, *Senex puerum
portabat*; Eccard, 'When to the
Temple Mary went.')
Marian antiphon at end of
Compline (until Maundy
Thursday - List B),
Ave regina coelorum.

ANNUNCIATION of the BVM   25 March (Lady Day; nine
months before Christ's birth):
Victoria, *In venisti enim
gratiam*, Schirmer, 1973.

St Mark   25 April.
SS Philip and James   1 May.
Invention of the Cross   3 May (finding of Cross by
Helena).

St Barnabas   11 June.
NATIVITY of St JOHN BAPTIST   24 June
St PETER and St PAUL   29 June. *Tu es Petrus* (Palestrina
à 4, Philips à 4+4).

St Mary Magdalene   22 July.
St James   25 July.
St Peter's Chains   1 August (also Lammas).
Transfiguration   6 August.
ASSUMPTION OF THE BVM   15 August (body and soul
assumed into heavenly glory).

St Bartholomew   24 August.
St Augustine (of Hippo)   28 August.
Beheading of St John Baptist   29 August.
NATIVITY OF BVM   8 September.
Exaltation of the Cross   14 September (recovery of
Cross from Persians).

St Matthew   21 September.
St Michael   29 September (Michaelmas).
St Luke   18 October.
SS Simon and Jude   28 October.

ALL SAINTS	1 November. Victoria, 'Glorious in Heaven' (*Gaudent in coelis*), *O quam gloriosum* (also Marenzio).
All Souls	2 November. *Justorum animae* (Byrd, Stanford).
St Catherine	25 November.

LIST B. **Lunar calendar**

Septuagesima	Third Sunday before Lent, ninth before Easter; 64 (not the nominal 70) days before Easter. Penitential season begins.
Sexagesima	A week later; *Exsurge* Sunday. Byrd, *Exsurge Domine*.
Quinquagesima	Fifty days from Easter (as in its name), counting Sundays.
Ash Wednesday	Forty days before Easter, not counting Sundays. Beginning of Lent.
Quadragesima	First Sunday in Lent, six weeks before Easter; gives its name to the 40 days of Lent.
Mothering Sunday	Fourth Sunday in Lent.
Passion Sunday	Fifth Sunday in Lent.
Holy Week:	
PALM SUNDAY	Sunday before Easter.
MAUNDY THURSDAY	
GOOD FRIDAY	
HOLY SATURDAY	
EASTER DAY	Marian antiphon at end of Compline (until Friday before Pentecost), *Regina caeli laetare*.
Low Sunday	Sunday after Easter. Byrd, *Post dies octo* (à 3, Annie Bank).

141

ASCENSION DAY	Forty days after Easter, counting Sundays including Easter, and so a Thursday. *Ascendit Deus* (Clemens, Philips); Byrd, *Psallite Domino*; Gibbons, 'O God, the King of Glory'.
PENTECOST (WHITSUN)	Fifty days (seven weeks) after Easter, counting similarly. Tallis, 'If ye love me'; Byrd, *Confirma hoc Deus; Non vos relinquam; Veni sancte Spiritus*; Palestrina, *Dum complerentur* (both parts).
TRINITY SUNDAY	Sunday after Pentecost (or Octave of Whitsun). Byrd, *O lux beata Trinitas; Tibi laus* (Lassus, Philips). Marian antiphon at first Vespers (until Saturday before Advent - List A), *Salve regina*.
CORPUS CHRISTI	Thursday after Trinity. *Ave verum corpus* (Byrd, Philips, Mozart); *O sacrum convivium* (Tallis, Byrd, Marenzio, Messiaen)
(Sundays after Trinity)	(From 22 to 27, depending on date of Easter. *ASB* uses Sundays after Pentecost.)

Note: 'Sundays after Epiphany' stop at Septuagesima in Anglican reckoning. In the Roman Catholic Church (1969) they are counted through the pre-Advent period but excluding Lent to Whitsun. *ASB* is the Church of England's *Alternative Service Book* (1980).

APPENDIX 2: WORDS AND ROLES
IN BACH'S *ST JOHN PASSION*

In Chapter 9 (pp. 109-11) I mentioned some problems which can be neglected in rehearsing this great work. Here I make suggestions about (A) the roles played by the crowd chorus as we go through the work; and the meaning of the German words in (B) the other choruses and the chorales, and (C) the solo arias and ariosos. The crowd's words and the recitatives can be followed in St John, 18 and 19.

In groups B and C the singers speak for the follower of Christ, and for the whole congregation of this Good Friday liturgy.

Bach's interpolations from St Matthew are found in no. 18, where the Evangelist tells us of Peter's bitter weeping, with echoes in 19 and 20; and the first of Matthew's two earthquakes and the tearing of the Temple veil (61, echoed in 62).

A. Who and where are the crowd, and where are we in the Gospel text?

The score of Bach's 'Passions' do not indicate whom the chorus and soloists are representing. That was obvious to his church singers, who were singing as part of a familiar liturgy. They may also have known the passion settings, with words by B.H. Brockes, where contemplative arias were sung by the Daughter of Zion, and responses by a chorus of Faithful Souls. All this is not so apparent to English-speaking singers. The following indications derive from notes I prepared for the Oxford Bach Choir.

Bach's text conflates the text of the Gospel; I have added signposts.

Number	St John (ch., v.)	Scene
3	18, 5	Brook Cedron (Gethsemane).
A band of men and officers		
from the chief priests and Pharisees.		

17	18, 17	High Priest's house.
Damsel keeping the door, and officers warming themselves.		

23	18, 30	Courtyard outside Governor's palace.
25	18, 31	do.
29	18, 40	do.
'The Jews' (chief priests and officers).		

34	19, 3	do.
The (Roman) soldiers.		

36	19, 6	do.
Chief priests and officers.		

38	19, 7	do.
42	19, 12	do.
44	19, 15	The Pavement (Gabbatha).
'The Jews' (chief priests and officers?).		

46	19, 15	do.
50	19, 21	Golgotha .
Chief priests.		

54	19, 24	do.
Soldiers.		

B. A literal translation of the German text of the other choruses.

English vocal scores do not always give much idea of what the German texts mean, partly because they have to be singable but also because German verse of the seventeenth and eighteenth centuries (see Chapter 9) leads to stronger phraseology than many now find comfortable (and the words themselves are sometimes antique). I do not think choirs realise the anguish and urgency of some of these: look at nos. 48 and 52, below. I offer these literal translations (owing much to discussions with Richard Jeffery) to choirs singing in English or in German. I have used familiar phrases where possible. The translations are not designed to be sung.

[In these numbers the chorus represents the Faithful Souls.]

1.   O Lord our Governor, how excellent is thy Name in all the world: (Ps. 8, 1: Bach however relates the words to Christ.)
Show through thy Passion that thou, the true Son of God, hast become glorified to all eternity, even in the lowest depths.

7.   O great and limitless love, which brought thee to this journey of agony: I lived in worldly pleasure and joy, and *thou* must suffer.

9.   Thy will be done on earth, as it is in heaven. Give us patience in time of sorrow, obedience in good times and bad; check and restrain all flesh and blood that acts against thy will.

15. Who has struck thee, my Saviour, and ill treated and tormented thee so? Thou art no sinner, like us and our children: thou knowest no misdeeds.

It is I, I and *my* sins, which are like grains of sand on the seashore, that brought thee this misery and this multitude of torments.

145

20. Peter impulsively denied his Lord: but once he had caught one grave glance he wept bitterly.

Jesu, look upon me too when I am unwilling to do penance: when I have done wrong, stir up my conscience.

21. Christ, who makes us blessed, did no evil: he was taken like a thief in the night, for our sakes, was led before a godless crowd, was subject to false accusations, mocked, jeered at and spat on - as Scripture says.

27. Ah great King, great to eternity, how can I do enough to make this faithfulness known? [Jesus has just said that his kingdom is not of this world, or his servants would have fought; he might have avoided suffering but chose not to.] The human mind cannot imagine what we can offer *thee*.

I cannot imagine what I can compare thy mercy with. How can my service repay thy deed of love?

40. Through *thy* imprisonment, Son of God, freedom has come to us.

Thy prison is our throne of grace, where all the godly can be free: without *thy* acceptance of bondage, our own would have been eternal.

48. [Bass solo:] Hurry, you tempted souls,
     away from your torment in hell -
[Chorus:] Where to? -
[Bass:] - to Golgotha! Accept wings of faith and flee -
[Chorus:] Where to?
[Bass:} - to the hill of the Cross:
     your weal [salvation] blossoms there.
               [Then first section again.]

52. In the depths of my heart, only thy Name and thy Cross gleam continually, and so I can be joyful. For comfort in my own need, may I see the image of thee, my kindest Lord Christ, bleeding to death.

56. He took good care of everything in his last hour, and was careful to find a guardian [John] for his mother. O man, do right, love God and man, and so die without death's torments, and let not your heart be troubled.

60. Jesu, thou that wast dead, livest now for all eternity: in my last death-throes do not turn me away to anywhere but to thee who didst atone for me. O my beloved Master, give me only what thou hast earned [our redemption through Christ's agony]. I do not desire more.

65. Help us, O Christ, Son of God, through thy bitter anguish, obediently to avoid all sin, fruitfully pondering thy death and its purpose, so that, however poor and weak, we can make thank-offering to thee.

67. Enjoy peace, you holy bones, which I now mourn no longer, and bring me - even me - to peace also.
    The grave which is appointed you [the bones], and which contains no more afflictions, opens my way to heaven and shuts the gates of hell.

68. Ah Lord, when my life finishes let thy dear angel carry my spirit to Abraham's bosom, and let my corpse rest easy in its little bedroom, without care or torment, until the Last Day.
    Then awaken me from death, so that my eyes see thee in all joy, O Son of God, my Saviour and my throne of grace.
    Lord Jesus Christ, grant my prayer: I will glorify thee for ever.

147

C. A literal translation of the arias and ariosos.

[The various soloists represent the Daughter of Zion, who
is the Church, the Bride of Christ.]

11. (Alto) To free me from the bonds of my sins, my Salvation
was bound; to heal me from all the sores of vice he himself was
willing to suffer hurt.

13. (Soprano) I follow thee likewise [like Simon Peter, no. 12]
with joyful steps, and will not leave thee, my Life and my Light.
Help me on my way, and do not cease to pull me, push me, and
beg me [to come].

19. (Tenor) Ah my mind, where do you want to go; where shall I
revive myself? Shall I stay here or do I wish for mountain and
hill on my back?
In the world there is no counsel, and my heart smarts with my
misdeed, because the servant has denied his Lord [Peter, no. 18].

31. (Bass) Ponder, my soul, with fearful pleasure, with bitter joy
and half-stifled heart, on your highest good, in Jesu's suffering.
Even as the key-of-heaven flower [cowslip, with its blood-like
spots] flowers out of [the crown of] thorns which prick Him, you
can pick much sweet fruit out of His wormwood: so gaze
without ceasing on him. (See p. v above.)

32. (Tenor) Consider how his blood-stained back in all its parts
becomes like Heaven; on it, after the waves of the Flood of our
sin have subsided, the most beautiful of rainbows appears as the
sign of God's grace.

48. (Bass and chorus) See p. 146.

58. (Alto) It is finished - O comfort for grieved souls. The night of sorrow lets me count its last hours.
The hero from out of Judah conquers with might and ends the struggle. It is finished.

60. (Bass; for chorus see B) My dear Saviour, let me ask you, as you are now nailed to the Cross, and yourself have said 'It is finished', have *I* been made free from death? Can I inherit the kingdom of heaven through your pain and dying? Is the salvation of all the world here?
You can indeed say nothing, because of your suffering: therefore you bow your head and silently say Yes.

62. (Tenor) My heart! while the whole world also suffers with Jesu's sufferings, the sun puts on mourning dress, the curtain is torn, the rocks crumble, the earth shakes, the graves are torn open, because they see the Creator grow cold [in death]. What will you [my heart] do, for your part?

APPENDIX 3
SERMON by Dr. JOHN MACQUARRIE:
JUDGMENT, HEAVEN AND HELL
(St Andrew's Church, Headington, 14 January 1996)

Now is the judgment of this world, now shall the ruler of this world be cast out; and I, when I am lifted up from the earth, will draw all men to myself. (John 12, 31f).

During the past week, the Doctrine Commission of the Church of England published its report on 'The Mystery of Salvation'. The document received quite a bit of attention in the newspapers. One ran a headline,'Church Still Believes in Hell', while another in more optimistic vein announced, 'Heaven's Gate Still Open'. Since some of you may have been confused by the media interpretations, I thought that today's sermon might profitably be devoted to clarifying our minds on some of the themes with which the Commission dealt, though we may not entirely agree with all its findings.

What happens to us after death? People have been wondering about that since prehistoric times, as witness the tombs that still exist from remote ages. But the simple and honest answer to the question is: No one knows. Not the bishops, not simple priests, not even the wise theologians at Christ Church. When Jesus himself was asked about the last day, he replied, 'Of that day or that hour, no one knows, not even the angels in heaven, nor the Son, but only the Father' (Mark 13, 32), and he contented himself with giving the practical advice,'Take heed, watch!' Shakespeare likewise reminds us of our ignorance, when Hamlet describes death as 'that undiscovered country from whose bourne no traveller returns'. No one comes back to tell us what lies on the other side.

But though we cannot know in the strict sense of having a clear and certain comprehension of what awaits us, Christians believe that by faith we can reach some understanding of human destiny. This faith is well founded. If indeed we human beings are made in the image of God, then God surely has a purpose for us that reaches beyond this world, a purpose that will be fulfilled when his image and likeness, which we so often sadly deface, will be brought to full and clear realisation in us his creatures. When that will happen and how it will happen, no one knows, not even in the high echelons of the C. of E.

But although Christians have often acknowledged that these matters are beyond the reach of human knowledge, they have told stories, formed imaginative pictures, used parables and metaphors, in attempts to express their faith that God himself cares for his people, both in this world and beyond. Our Lord himself told parables about the last things. Partly out of the Bible but also from the vivid imaginations of poets and preachers, from the creations of painters and the speculations of philosophers and pseudo-philosophers, a popular mythology was constructed and was often taken in a literal sense. There would be a day of judgment, and its solemn proceedings would be very like those of a human law-court; the reward of the faithful would be the privilege of living in heaven, conceived also in very earthly terms, with streets of gold and every kind of magnificence; and for those declared guilty there would be a miserable existence in hell, where they would be subjected to scorching heat and other torments. All this would take place in the future, and increasingly this was conceived as a distant future. These ideas may have been very vivid and realistic to people in the early years of the Church; they continued to be influential in the Middle Ages, when Dante wrote his great poem describing heaven, purgatory and hell; even as recently as Victorian times, preachers sometimes terrified their congregations with hell-fire sermons.

But all this was bound to fade in course of time, for not only was it projected into some indefinite and remote future, it seemed also to be in conflict with scientific conceptions of time, space and the cosmos. Contrast with this elaborate and now discredited mythology the words of Jesus which we have taken as a text: 'Now is the judgment of this world, now shall the ruler of this world be cast out'. The emphasis is on the now. Jesus brings the idea of judgment from the distant future into the present, from the realms of imagination into everyday experience.

And I think it follows that if we accept that 'Now is the judgment of this world', we may go on to accept that now we may have experience of heaven, now we may know the reality of hell, now is taking place that process of purgation whereby men and women are being prepared for communion with God. Our minds are withdrawn from visions of the future to the realities of the present, where, according to our Lord, we can already know the judgment of God, the joy of his love and the pain of separation from him. Now is the judgment of this world! Not just after death, not at some remote time in the never never, but now, day by day, in the moral decisions that men and women everywhere are taking, including you and me, judgment is going on. We are being judged in the light of Jesus Christ, himself the human being in whom the image of God was fully manifested.

If we have seen in him the goal of human life, then we can understand why, after speaking of the judgment of this world, he went on to say that when he was lifted up, he would draw all people to himself. The nearer we draw to him, the more we become aware of the good purpose for which God has created us, and the more we become aware that we are under judgment. And as we slip back from Christ or deny him, we are aware that we are condemning ourselves and destroying ourselves.

So we begin to understand more clearly what heaven and hell are. They are not places 'out there' where on some far-off date we may arrive. They are rather states of our souls or selves, in which even now we learn who we really are. So far as we are being conformed to Christ, growing into his likeness, we are gaining our true selves. Heaven is not some external reward, some bonus that we get for having tried to follow Christ: heaven is the Christian life itself, a life of love, truth, faithfulness, communion, a life drawn from God's own life. When Jesus says that if he is lifted up, all people will be drawn to him, the evangelist adds an explanation of what he meant: 'He said this, to show by what death he should die'. The lifting up is the lifting up on the cross. He did not mean his exaltation in heaven at the end of all time, but his death as his supreme act of self-giving love. The reward of living the Christian life is simply to be able more fully to manifest his love.

And just as heaven is not an external reward but the life-deepening discipleship itself, so hell is not an external punishment, but just the working-out of sin in human life. Just as the following of Jesus helps us to become our true selves as children of God, so the following of our sinful and self-centred tendencies makes us less than we might be, diminishes us and may eventually break up and destroy us.

It is not God who prepares a hell for the wicked: men and women make their own hells, the self-inflicted hells that are the consequences of sin. Dante in his famous poem showed how each sin is its own punishment as it takes hold on a person. In one part of hell, he tells us how he saw men wearing gorgeous robes, but moving only with great pain and difficulty. These are the hypocrites, and Dante explains that their beautiful robes were lined with lead which dragged them down so that they could hardly move. They had built up an outward show of goodness, but then they were constantly in terror that they might in an unguarded moment reveal what they really were. In another part of hell, Dante saw people who were being blown about by gale-

force winds, torn and crushed. They were the lustful, the victims of their own undisciplined passions, and again we see that the punishment is nothing but the sin itself. Hell is not the dreadful penalty exacted by a stern vengeful God. It is the working out in ourselves and in society of human sins, greed, aggression, indiscipline and all the rest. Even if there were no God, there would still be hell, the hell we inflict on ourselves.

But if there were no God, there would be no heaven, no final hope for the human race. One of Dostoyevsky's characters asked: 'If there is no God, then is everything permitted?' We boast nowadays of the 'permissive society', but if there are no ultimate standards to guide us, is there a danger that we may be following the way to hell?

Many people nowadays laugh at the idea of hell, and that is not surprising, considering the ways in which hell has been traditionally pictured. But hell is a reality, and we ought to fear hell. To ignore hell or to deny it is to come very close to denying that there is any moral government of the universe, and that is a very dangerous step to take. In one of our Lord's parables, he compares the world to a field in which good wheat and weeds are growing together. Not just the world, but each one of us, is like that field. No one has ever satisfactorily explained where the weeds have come from.There is a mystery of evil in the creation, and we do not know how to account for it. But much of that evil, many of the weeds in the field, are due to human agency and the consequences which they bring we bring upon ourselves. We cannot solve the problems of the universe, but we do have a responsibility in those matters where the human factor is decisive. By following Christ and by using the means of grace, we can do something to ensure that, so far as we can, the good grain will grow and the weeds wither away. So let us hear Christ's warning and invitation: 'Now is the judgment of this world. ... And I, if I be lifted up, will draw all men to myself'.

APPENDIX 4:
HERESIES AND THE CREEDS

In the early days of the Church, under Roman oppression, people wishing to be baptised and received as members were required to make in public the affirmation 'Jesus is Lord'. This was both a guarantee of their serious intentions and a safeguard against infiltration by spies, since a Roman agent would not, it was assumed, deny the lordship of Caesar (regarded as divine). As the Church spread through the Eastern Mediterranean seaboard, where the common tongue was Greek, local variants were adopted; theologians had to meet questions arising from a Greek philosophical attitude which was different from the Jewish approach to religion.

Rome had become a principal centre of the Church by the second century, and their form of the baptismal vow was widely adopted, and much later (the eighth century) emerged as our Apostles' Creed. This is the creed found in the *Book of Common Prayer* under 'Morning Prayer', after the canticle following the Second Lesson, and in the same position under 'Evening Prayer'.

Arianism

Some theologians argued as follows: 'If Jesus Christ was the Son of the Father, was he not created at the moment of his conception and birth? If so, he did not exist from all eternity, and he cannot be wholly divine. The Holy Spirit likewise was created, by the Son, at a later date. Christ must have been demi-God and demi-man.' This doctrine had serious support (which continued for some centuries), but it was attacked as a form of polytheism, not clearly different from the old Roman pagan religion which both the Church and (since 313) the Emperor Constantine wanted to remove. There was sharp religious strife on the point, and danger of political instability in the Empire, under attack by northern 'barbarians', and with repeated civil war between rival Emperors (in 330 Constantine founded his New Rome at Constantinople). Constantine called a Council of the Church at Nicaea in 325, and took the chair (although not yet baptised); and a short Creed, in Greek, was agreed by many though not all of the bishops. This denied the Arian doctrine by saying that Christ was begotten of the Father, not made, and was of one essence with the Father (in Latin, *consubstantialem Patri*). But the dispute continued. Athanasius led the pro-Nicene party (see below for his Creed); in 381 the Emperor Theodosius, in charge of a re-united Empire, called a Council at Constantinople. The resulting Nicaeno-Constantinopolitan Creed is our 'Nicene Creed' - except that the Western Church later added to the statement about the Holy Spirit that it proceeds from the Father *and the Son* (*filioque*). It settled for the Church the argument about the Arian heresy. A further argument about how Christ could be both God and man was settled at a Council at Chalcedon in 451; the results were not accepted by some Eastern Churches, and the Creed was not amended.

The text of the 'Nicene Creed' makes repeated assertions so as to make sure Arianism had no toe-hold left:

Et in unum Dominum Iesum Christum,
   filium Dei unigenitum
   et ex Patre natum ante omnia saecula,
   Deum de Deo, lumen de lumine,
5   *Deum verum de Deo vero,*
   genitum non factum,

consubstantialem Patri,
per quem omnia facta sunt:

In line 1 of this passage Christ is one Lord not one of three Lords. In lines 2-3 he was born before all worlds, not at some date like 4 BC. In lines 4-5 he is God of (or from) God, light out of light, true God from the true God. Line 6 makes sure we know he was not made, but begotten, and line 7 that he was of one substance with the Father (or of one *essence,* which in Greek philosophy was what made things what they are). So he was fully divine, as well as fully human - *et incarnatus est ... et homo factus est* - since he performed the earthly deeds which the Creed goes on to enumerate. Moreover, the Creed goes on to say *per quem omnia facta sunt:* everything was made through the Word, the *Logos,* who became flesh in Jesus Christ (thus confirming that the Second Person of the Trinity already existed at the Creation, whatever the Arians might say).

The text of the 'Nicene Creed' appears in the Masses we sing; the modern English (or other vernacular) version comes after the sermon (which follows the Gospel reading) in contemporary Anglican or Roman Catholic service books. The text used in the *Book of Common Prayer* (where the Communion service is tucked away towards the end of the book) has been revised: for instance, 'seen and unseen' replaces 'visible and invisible'.

Filioque and other subtleties

The *filioque* addition (see p. 156) was not and still is not accepted by the Eastern (Orthodox) Churches. With other matters such as the supremacy of the Pope, the date of Easter, and the marriage of Orthodox clergy, it prevents union or even inter-communion between Catholic and Orthodox Churches.

A member of the Anglican or Roman Church has to accept the Creed and solemnly affirm it. Yet how many worshippers in either church have a view on the details of these matters, rather than just accepting the wisdom of their own authorities? Not only is the affirmation a guarantee of conflict over a point which is not of live concern to the worshipper, but it is an indication that the Creed may include several other clauses which cause concern to many people who are serious about religion; the Virgin birth and the resurrection of the body are obvious examples. I find even more troublesome the idea that one should solemnly affirm these difficult and controversial doctrines without understanding and fully accepting them (and this prevents me from seeking membership of the Church of England: I am grateful to have been accepted for some years past as a regular, though non-conformist, communicant visitor).

Modern interpretations and Apostolic doctrine

I know that many attempts have been made to produce acceptable modern meanings to the Creed; a short book-list below mentions a few. But they run up against a further objection. The Creed is held up as an essential element of continuity of doctrine from early times, which guarantees the authenticity and authority of the present Church. But if the early Fathers demanded belief in the resurrection of the flesh (later, 'body'), and we liberalise the doctrine to make it credible today, we cannot also claim that we are preserving apostolic doctrine. This would not trouble me; we have to use the abilities God gave us to find and express his truth and guidance in our changing world, and I do not think it is sensible to try to decree a universal doctrine, let alone one that will last for ever.

Nevertheless the Church is right to expect that members will be serious in intention and not follow false Christs - a problem that was already familiar to Jesus; his concluding advice was 'Wherefore by their fruits ye shall know them' (Matthew 7, 15-20). This seems very sensible to the pragmatic English mind: but on what do we base our value-judgments? We must be able to derive these from Christ's own teaching, not simply accept those which come out of the teaching of the new prophet in question. And we have to avoid falling into a sterile fundamentalist adherence to favourite Biblical texts. It is all very difficult!

The Creeds give us no guidance about Christian doctrine or behaviour; in particular, there is nothing of 'This is my commandment, That ye love one another, as I have loved you' (John 15, 12). Nor could someone considering joining the Church get an idea from the Creed about what the Church might offer, even on the Church's sacraments. My own preference is for an affirmation by church members on the lines of that used in 'The Nature, Faith and Order of the United Reformed Church'. Its Confession of Faith, read by the Minister presiding, begins with a statement of general Trinitarian belief, followed by acceptance of 'the witness to the catholic faith in the Apostles' and Nicene Creeds.' Then the declarations made by those who united as the URC (Congregationalists, Presbyterians and Churches of Christ) are acknowledged, and the people respond with 'Faith alive and active: gift of an eternal source, renewed for every generation'. Still more specifically, '... we affirm our right and readiness, if the need arises, to ... make new statements of faith in ever new obedience to the Living Christ.' (*Rejoice and Sing*, Oxford, 1991, 851-3.)

Heresies

For convenience I add a list of some heresies other than Arianism. Readers may feel that these are not ridiculous ideas: indeed, they were seriously held by educated and well-read Christians. The relevant entries in the *Oxford Dictionary of the Christian Church* indicate where detailed examination can be found.

Arianism leads into **Nestorianism** (Christ's deity separate from his humanity). It is opposed by **Apollinarianism**, 'the first great Christological heresy', according to which there was unity of Godhead and manhood in Christ, who had full deity but whose moral life did not develop; the spirit which exists in man was replaced by the divine Logos, so Christ lacked complete manhood, so he could not be a perfect example to us and only redeemed the spiritual part of our nature.

Monophysitism holds that Christ had a single, divine, nature, so after his incarnation was not both divine and human. (**Docetism** had similarly held that Christ's humanity was apparent, not real, and likewise his sufferings.)

Manichaeism, an ascetic form of Gnosticism (which claimed special knowledge of ultimate reality), held that matter was evil, spirit good, and worked out a cosmic system to release the light which, they taught, Satan had stolen. It has been called the 'Pauline heresy' (perhaps unfairly, but we can see the tendency in 'Ye are not of the flesh, but of the Spirit' in 'Jesu, priceless Treasure': Romans 8, 9). The attitude of Western religion to the body, to enjoyment and particularly towards sex as being unclean, comes out of this tendency; in turn it requires a theology involving a virgin birth and a mother who had not engaged in the activities normally regarded as necessary for having a child.

Three groups of heretics with doctrines connected with Manichaeanism, all suppressed with immense cruelty by the Catholic powers in the twelfth and thirteenth centuries, were the **Bogomils**, the **Cathari** and the **Albigensians** (centred in Albi, southern France). The *Oxford Dictionary of the Christian Church* describes their respective beliefs.

Pelagianism held that man can himself take the fundamental steps to salvation without depending on divine grace. Pelagius was a British theologian who taught in Rome around AD 400. After long arguments his ideas were declared heretical, but they lingered for many centuries in Britain and Gaul. Some of his followers also denied the transmission of original sin to us from Adam.

So what happens to us if we hold any of these heresies, or believe nothing? This is explained in the Athanasian Creed, which is accepted (reluctantly) in the Western Church but not in the Eastern Orthodox Churches.

The 'Athanasian' Creed

After the *Book of Common Prayer* has shown us Morning Prayer and Evening Prayer we find 'At Morning Prayer', and the instruction to sing or say on thirteen named occasions in the year, instead of the Apostles' Creed, 'this Confession of our Christian Faith, commonly called The Creed of Saint Athanasius, ... Quicunque Vult'. This instruction is very widely ignored: but what's the good of a Creed if you don't say it as instructed? It is designed (a generation or two after Athanasius's death in AD 373) to state doctrine and remove heresy, and readers may like to

161

be reminded of its remarkable language. I will quote the beginning and the end:

Whosoever will be saved: before all things it is necessary that he hold the Catholick Faith.
Which Faith except every one do keep whole and undefiled: without doubt he shall perish everlastingly.
And the Catholick Faith is this ...
[2½ pages follow]
And they that have done good shall go into life everlasting: and they that have done evil into everlasting fire.
This is the Catholick Faith: which except a man believe faithfully, he cannot be saved.

Can one wonder that people with a real fear of the hereafter came to church and obediently toed the line? Or that they stopped coming as soon as hellfire was soft-pedalled for the modern world? This is fine traditional doctrine but it speaks not at all of the redemptive and creative love which is at the heart of Christianity as we now see it. Attempts to remove it have long been thwarted by those who fear the dilution of traditional doctrine.

Incidentally, does not the penultimate paragraph quoted above excuse simple-minded folk who thought they could get to heaven by good deeds ('works') rather than by God's grace and choice, as the Protestant reformation affirmed?

APPENDIX 5:
MASS, OFFICE AND
ANGLICAN SERVICES -

STRUCTURE OF THE LITURGY.

This note has a very limited purpose: to suggest to those who are mainly familiar with polyphonic settings of the Ordinary of the Mass and of motets, and with English service settings and anthems, how they can start to understand the vastly complex liturgical background. Rather than write an introduction to the liturgy, which would require a degree of understanding I do not pretend to, I shall provide an introduction to an introduction. We can be grateful that this latter is conveniently available in an Oxford paperback: John Harper, *The Forms and Orders of Western Liturgy from the Tenth to the Eighteenth Century: A Historical Introduction and Guide for Students and Musicians*. I will shorten this formidable title to 'Harper', and pull some themes out of it to supplement what I have written in Chapters 4, 6, 8 and 9; Professor Harper is not however to be held responsible for anything I write. I shall say many things which a devout church-goer in either the Roman or the Anglican tradition will regard as too obvious to be said: but I know that many singers do not have that experience but do have open and enquiring minds.

There are four broad periods in the history of the liturgy:

i. the early Church, particularly the times of the Greek Fathers of the Church, the early Church in Rome and the beginnings of monasticism, followed by the disruptive invasions from the north in the fifth century;

ii. the medieval Church, during and after the recovery from those invasions: we can think of 800 as a convenient date,

iii. the post-Reformation Churches; and

iv. the modern Churches, since the move towards a form of Mass or Eucharist, in the vernacular, where Anglican and Roman Catholic services are very similar: this dates from the Second Vatican Council (1962) and some years before that in the Church of England.

The polyphonic music and the great structure of 'Gregorian' chant belong to periods ii and iii. The relevant types of service are
(ii) the **Office** based on Benedictine monastic usage but followed also in 'secular' churches; and the **medieval Mass**, for which there were a variety of Uses in different countries and regions;
(iii) the **Tridentine Mass**, emerging in 1570 after the Council of Trent, simplified and standardised for the whole of the Catholic world under Roman supervision; the Office (out of which **Vespers** became the most important: Harper, 158f); and the Reformed or semi-reformed liturgies, in the Anglican *Book of Common Prayer* (1549, revised at various dates including 1662) and - not covered in this note - those developed by Lutheran, Calvinist, and other Protestant churches.

The Office

The word 'office' has the sense of service and duty; the Divine Office is the daily round of prayer; in the services (in the modern sense of that word) the members of a community serve God in worship, and fulfil the duty arising from their membership. (For the Mass see below.) In the Middle Ages the greater 'secular' churches followed the monasteries in performing Matins in the night, with Lauds immediately following, or else at dawn; then Prime, Terce, Sext and None; Vespers at dusk; and Compline before sleeping. In the centuries after the Reformation many monasteries survived, though in some countries they were dissolved (England and Scotland) or prohibited (France, after the Revolution).

The centre of the Office services was the recitation of the Psalms (Harper ch. 5), as in the early Church and indeed in Jewish worship, particularly in the Temple. Usually these were chanted, in Latin, and from memory. There was a limited amount of other Scripture reading, and there were hymns like *Christe qui lux es et dies* ('O Christ who art the light and day'), often in four-line stanzas, rhythmic (not normally classically quantitative) and using rhyme. The Office is covered in Harper, ch. 6, with a broad summary table on 76f.

The Medieval Mass

The Mass, or Eucharist, was (and still is) the principal act of worship in the Catholic Church. 'Mass' derives, through *missa*, from the Latin for 'to send'. In this sacrament the priest consecrates bread and wine which he consumes (in the Communion) as Christ's body and blood in commemoration and re-enactment of His sacrifice on the Cross. The faithful in the congregation, who were observers only but had confessed their sins, 'have remission of pain or guilt'. In Roman Catholic doctrine the Mass is not a commemoration or memorial; Christ's presence is real; in terms of medieval philosophy transubstantiation has taken place - an idea, which I am not competent to elucidate, which has caused bitter strife for centuries. (Article of Religion XXXI in the *BCP* says that these were 'blasphemous fables, and dangerous deceits'.)

Harper, ch. 7, explains the structure of the medieval High Mass. There were fewer regional 'Uses' than for the Office, and the general shape is recognisable from the post-Reformation (Tridentine) and modern masses. (The parts of the text and chant of the Mass which remain unchanged through the year are the Ordinary - principally the *Kyrie, Gloria, Credo, Sanctus, Benedictus*, and *Agnus*. The changing parts are the Proper.)

After an Introit the *Kyrie* and *Gloria in excelsis* are sung by the choir, the Epistle is read (intoned), the Gradual (followed by an Alleluia and a Sequence) is sung to mark the move of the Deacon to the steps (*gradus*) from which he will read the Gospel. The *Credo* follows, though this was only included in the Mass from the tenth century. Then the Offertory is sung, as the offerings of bread and wine are taken to the altar. The celebrant intones the Preface to the Eucharistic prayer at the altar, and the choir sing the *Sanctus* and *Benedictus*; particularly from this point the choir's singing cannot be co-ordinated with the (inaudible) words of the celebrant, who is some distance away, facing the altar. He continues with the Canon of the Mass, the prayer in which he blesses and consecrates the 'elements' which are to become Christ's body; a bell is rung at the blessing and at the elevation of the Host, the sanctified bread. The Lord's Prayer follows, then the *Pax* (Versicle

'The peace of the Lord be always with you.' Response 'And with thy spirit'), the *Agnus Dei*, and the Rite of Peace. The priest then takes Communion by consuming the consecrated bread and wine; a communion antiphon is sung. After a prayer the celebrant dismisses the people with *Ite, missa est* (a compressed phrase which may be translated as 'Go, the Mass has now been sent to you').

Polyphony was heard only in churches with trained singers, and even then there was much singing in the form of chant by the celebrant priest, the deacon or the choir, and the liturgy includes much movement through the choir and sanctuary and very many details of action by priests, servers and choir with their own religious significance; some of this, particularly the use of incense and the general impression of colour and movement, was apparent to the people standing, without a part to play, in the nave.

At Low Mass, the most common form of celebration, a single priest read the service, with no singing (see *ODCC*).

To attempt reconstructions of medieval or later liturgies is a highly expert affair - even if such an attempt is deemed appropriate: see discussion in *Early Music Review*, March 1996. Harper gives guidance in chapters 12 and 13, supplemented by ch. 8 on additional observances such as processions, ch. 9 on Holy Week and Easter, and ch. 4 on liturgical books.

Harper has a full and indispensable Glossary (286-319).

The Tridentine Mass

Harper's ch. 9 explains the changes made in 1570 after the Council of Trent, and the deliberate move towards centralisation and uniformity as well as comparative simplicity, with an emphasis on the clarity of the words to be sung. Polyphony of the modified kind became more prevalent: more was being composed and there were more trained singers and rich patrons to finance the choral establishments.

Most of the music written for the Tridentine Mass is continental, though Byrd's later motets and his Masses were so intended. In its early years it was also in part international, through the movements of professional musicians between the Low Countries, Italy, Germany and Spain.

An account of the **Requiem Mass**, and the variations in well-known settings, with translations, is in I. Trusler, *The Choral Director's Latin* (NY and London, 1987), 46-64.

Vespers

Outside the remaining monasteries the main survivor of the Office was Vespers (Harper, 158-61). Non-specialists can perhaps best follow the great developments in Monteverdi's time by studying articles and correspondence in *Early Music*, and scholarly sleeve-notes: there has been controversy about what to include in a performance, as well as on musical matters such as pitch (*Early Music*, P. McCreesh, May 1995, 325, and A. Parrott, November 1984, 490). It was the elaboration of Vespers that specially concerned Pope Pius X in 1903 in his reforming *Motu proprio* (see my *Singing in Latin*, 301).

The Book of Common Prayer

The Act of Uniformity of 1549, in Edward VI's reign, ordered the exclusive use of a new prayer book in public worship, in English (with permission for services in Latin, Greek and Hebrew in the universities and certain schools). This had been prepared under Archbishop Cranmer's guidance; after various disputes it was revised in 1552, 1559

and 1662 (the present book, a 1927-8 revision having failed
to win parliamentary approval). An Act of 1965 allowed
other liturgies to be tried out, and these led to the wide use
of the *Alternative Service Book* (*ASB*), 1980, whose Eucharist
and the reformed vernacular Roman Catholic service are,
for ecumenical reasons, deliberately similar.

Cranmer constructed the services of Morning and
Evening Prayer (Matins and Evensong) from the Latin
Office, mainly from Matins, Vespers and Compline; the
exact correspondence is set out in Harper, 172-4. The
Communion service, superseding the Mass (although that
word has crept back through Anglo-Catholic influence), is
on his pages 181f; it often followed Matins, and some of the
congregation might leave before the Communion. *Kyrie
eleison* is replaced by the response after each of the Ten
Commandments 'Lord, have mercy upon us, and incline
our hearts to keep this law'. 'Glory be to God on high'
comes near the end of this service, whereas *Gloria in excelsis*
is sung near the beginning of the Mass and the modern
Parish Communion. The Priest includes 'Holy, Holy, Holy'
in the Eucharistic Prayer, but *Benedictus* and *Agnus Dei* are
not represented in the Prayer Book service.

Most of the Anglican church music until recent years
was written for Matins and Evensong - a rich collection of
'service settings' (of the canticles) and anthems, together
with *Preces* and Responses for priest and choir. Anglican
chant, designed to succeed plainsong, was written for the
psalms, which are sung in a monthly cycle appearing in the
Prayer Book; for instance, Ps. 78 is sung on the 15th
Evening (the most strenuous of the month, as there are 73
verses). The psalms are customarily sung antiphonally by
the choir in a cathedral-type service; otherwise they may be
sung or said by all present.

BIBLIOGRAPHY

This list shows details of books mentioned in the text (except a few whose details have been given), and a few other background books which readers may find helpful. It is not a summary of the vast range of writing on the subjects covered.

History, language, liturgy, music
Aston, M., *Faith and Fire*, London, 1971.
Chadwick, H., *Early Christian Thought and the Classical Tradition*, Oxford, 1984.
Copeman, H., *Singing in Latin*, Oxford, pb., 1992.
Duffy, E., *The Stripping of the Altars*, New Haven and London, 1992.
Fellowes, E.H., *William Byrd*, Oxford, 1936.
Frazer, J.G., *The Golden Bough*, London, 1923.
Harper, J., *The Forms and Orders of Western Liturgy from the Tenth to the Eighteenth Century*, Oxford pb., 1991.
Harrison, F.L., *Music in Medieval Britain*, London, 1963.
Harrán, D., *In Search of Harmony*, Stuttgart, 1988.
Lewis, C.S., *The Allegory of Love*, Oxford, 1936.
Morley, T., *A Plain and Easy Introduction to Practical Music*, modern edn., London, 1952.
Robinson, E., *The Language of Mystery*, London, 1987.
Routley, E.,
    Hymns and Human Life, London, 1952, 2nd edn. 1959.
    Hymns and the Faith, London, 1955.
    Hymns Today and Tomorrow, US, 1964, London, 1966.
    The English Carol, London, 1958.
Soskice, J.M., *Metaphor and Religious Language* , Oxford, 1985.
Strohm, R., *Music in Late Medieval Bruges*, Oxford, rev. pb., 1990.
Taruskin, R., *Text and Act*, NY and Oxford, 1995.
Talley, T.J., *The Origins of the Liturgical Year*, N Y., 1986.
Thomas, K., *Religion and the Decline of Magic*, pb., London, 1971.

BIBLIOGRAPHY

Temperley, N., *The Music of the English Parish Church*, Cambridge, 1979.
Williams, H.A., *True Resurrection*, London, 1972.
Young, K., *The Drama of the Medieval Church*, Oxford, 1933.

The Bible, the Creeds, etc.
Revised English Bible, Oxford and Cambridge, 1989.
Oxford Dictionary of the Christian Church (ODCC), Oxford, 1974 edn., revised reprints.
Barth, K., *Dogmatics in outline*, tr. London, 1949. An exciting Protestant book, but long obscure passages.
Charpentier, E., *How to read the New Testament*, London, 1981. A French Catholic guide.
Davies, R.E., *Making Sense of the Creeds*, London, 1987. A Methodist minister's account.
Fenton, J., *Finding the Way through John*, London, 1995. *The St Matthew Passion*, Oxford, 1995.
Küng, H., *Credo*, tr. London, 1993. A modern Catholic view.
Macquarrie, J., *Jesus Christ in Modern Thought*, London, 1990.
Wilson, A., *Jesus*, London, 1993.

Carol books referred to:
Oxford Book of Carols, Oxford, 1928.
New Oxford Book of Carols, Oxford, 1992.
Shorter New Oxford Book of Carols, Oxford, 1993.

Shape-note singing:
Gordon, Larry, ed., *Northern Harmony*, Plainfield, Vermont.

INDEX

173

INDEX